PERGAMON INSTITUTE OF ENGLISH (NEW YORK)

Language Teaching Methodology Series

The Communicative Syllabus
Evolution,
Design and Implementation

Other titles in this series include:

ALTMAN, Howard B. and C. Vaughan James
Foreign Language Teaching: meeting individual needs

BRUMFIT, Christopher J.
Problems and Principles in English Teaching

BRUMFIT, Christopher J.
English for International Communication

CARROLL, Brendan J.
Testing Communicative Performance: an interim study

FISIAK, Jacek (ed)
Contrastive Linguistics and the Language Teacher

FREUDENSTEIN, BENEKE, PONISH (eds)
Language Incorporated: teaching foreign languages in industry

FREUDENSTEIN, Reinhold
Teaching Foreign Languages to the Very Young

JOHNSON, Keith
Communicative Syllabus Design and Methodology

JUNG, Udo
Reading: a symposium

KELLERMAN, Marcelle
The Forgotten Third Skill: reading a foreign language

KRASHEN, Stephen
Second Language Acquisition and Second Language Learning

KRASHEN, Stephen
Principles and Practice in Second Language Acquisition

KRASHEN, Stephen and Tracy Terrell
The Natural Approach

LEONTIEV, Alexei
Psychology and the Language Learning Process

LOVEDAY, Leo
The Sociolinguistics of Learning and Using a Non-native Language

ROBINSON, Pauline C.
ESP (English for Specific Purposes)

SHARP, Derrick W. H.
English at School: the wood and the trees

STREVENS, Peter
Teaching English as an International Language

TOSI, Arturo
Immigration and Bilingual Education

See also SYSTEM *the international journal of Educational Technology and Language Learning Systems* (sample copy available on request).

The Communicative Syllabus
Evolution,
Design and Implementation

JANICE YALDEN

Centre for Applied Language Studies,
Carleton University, Ottawa, Canada

PERGAMON PRESS

Oxford · New York · Toronto · Sydney · Paris · Frankfurt

U.K.	Pergamon Press Ltd., Headington Hill Hall, Oxford OX3 0BW, England
U.S.A.	Pergamon Press Inc., Maxwell House, Fairview Park, Elmsford, New York 10523, U.S.A.
CANADA	Pergamon Press Canada Ltd., Suite 104, 150 Consumers Rd., Willowdale, Ontario M2J 1P9, Canada
AUSTRALIA	Pergamon Press (Aust.) Pty. Ltd., P.O. Box 544, Potts Point, N.S.W. 2011, Australia
FRANCE	Pergamon Press SARL, 24 rue des Ecoles, 75240 Paris, Cedex 05, France
FEDERAL REPUBLIC OF GERMANY	Pergamon Press GmbH, Hammerweg 6, D-6242 Kronberg-Taunus, Federal Republic of Germany

First edition 1983

Library of Congress Cataloging in Publication Data

Yalden, Janice.
The communicative syllabus.
(Language teaching methodology series)
Bibliography: p.
Includes index.
1. Languages, Modern—Study and teaching. 2. Curriculum planning. 3. Communicative competence. I. Title.
II. Series.
PB36.Y34   1983   418'.007'07   82-11244

British Library Cataloguing in Publication Data

Yalden, Janice
The communicative syllabus. — (Language teaching methodology series)
I. Title II. Series
418'.007'1   PB36
ISBN 0-08-028615-1

Printed in Great Britain by A. Wheaton & Co. Ltd., Exeter

For
Max, Robert and Cicely

Acknowledgements

The author and publisher are grateful for permission to reproduce matter from the following sources:

Alexander, L. G. (1978) *Some Methodological Implications of Waystage and Threshold Level.* Council of Europe, Strasbourg, (Grid)

Allen, J. P. B. (1980) *A Three-level Curriculum Model for Second-Language Education.* Mimeo: Modern Language Centre, Ontario Institute for Studies in Education, (Figure on page 114)

Allen, P. (1977) *TESL Talk, Vol. 8, No. 1 (Jan),* "Structural and Functional Models in Language Teaching," (Figure on page 9)

Brumfit, C. J. (1980) "Communicative Specification vs. Communicative Methodology," in *Studies in Second-Language Acquisition,* **3,** Bloomington, Ind. (Figure on page 112)

Dixson, R. J. (1973) *Modern American English,* Book I, (Revised edn) Reproduced by permission of Centre Educatif et Culturel, Montreal, Canada, (Table of contents)

Lado, R. (1970) *Lado English Studies,* Book I, (Students' Book), (Table of contents)

Praninskas, J. (1975) *Rapid Review of English Grammar,* (2nd. edn) Reproduced by permission of Prentice-Hall, Inc. Englewood Cliffs, N.J. (Table of contents)

Mackay, R. "Practical Curriculum Development and Evaluation in ESP/EST" in *ESP Newsletter Issue 20,* (Figure 5 and 6 on pages 88, 98 adapted)

Maley, A. (1980) "Teaching for Communicative Competence" in *Studies in Second-Language Acquisition,* **3,** Bloomington, Ind. (Figure on page 116)

Strevens, P. (1978) "Special Purpose Language Teaching: A Perspective," *Language Teaching and Linguistics: Abstracts.* II: p. 156

Foreword

THIS volume provides a comprehensive discussion of syllabus design from a North American point of view. It demonstrates the importance of this field for the language-program planner and language teacher, in view of two converging currents of thought: North American psycholinguistic studies and European work on the needs survey and the notional syllabus.

Part One, The Background to Syllabus Design, begins with a review of changes in linguistic theory which have a particular relevance to the work of the applied linguist in his role as designer of language syllabuses. The areas touched on are interlanguage studies, neurolinguistics, current work in second-language acquisition including Krashen's Monitor Theory, as well as recent theories of language as communication. In other words the discussion in the first chapter is structured around current views of what language is and how it is acquired, and resulting implications for the adult learning a second language. The work then moves on to define the term 'syllabus' and to characterize the traditional approach to syllabus design. The concept of an alternative model—the semantic syllabus—is introduced. Structural, situational and notional syllabuses are identified, their salient features are described, and an evolutionary pattern is established.

Chapter 2, on context and function, clarifies the theoretical currents which gave rise to the notional syllabus, through a discussion of European functional theories of meaning and of language. But this is preceded by an analysis of the change of emphasis in North American language teaching theory, from a formalist approach to one which is based on the question of *how* a learner acquires a second language. It is shown that this interest in the psychology of the second-language learner is by no means incompatible with emphasis on the learner as a social being, on *why* he acquires a second language. The conjoining of interests, however, must lead to an examination of the question of the functions of language, and of how to account for them in second-language teaching. For this reason, it is argued that an understanding of Prague school linguistics and of British linguistics will assist the syllabus designer in his work.

Approaches to the problems of the second-language learner, contributed by linguists on both sides of the Atlantic, thus serve as background to a description in Chapters 3 and 4 of the Council of Europe Modern Languages Project, and of subsequent work in syllabus theory in Britain. The number of components in a semantic syllabus is seen to have greatly increased, and the issue of the addition of the component of discourse structure is taken up. Finally, a five-step model of the communicative process is adopted for the purposes of the present work.

The thesis of the book is that the 'method' concept has failed; nevertheless the teacher is responsible for providing guidance to the learner who for the most part is not able to act autonomously, particularly in the early stages. This guidance can best be decided on through a needs survey and choice of an appropriate syllabus type, rather than choice of any one method. It is quite possible to retain concern for the learner *qua* individual and at the same time exploit information gathered via the needs survey to generate a large amount of high-interest teaching material for any given group of learners. Part Two is therefore a treatment of the processes involved in planning and developing a communicative syllabus. Emphasis throughout is on the preparation of language-teaching programs and courses for adolescents and adults.

In Chapter 5 a general description of several phases of language program development is provided, followed in Chapter 6 by an analysis of current syllabus types. Six broad categories are established. The presentation of the 'proportional' approach to syllabus design, which synthesizes the several versions of the input syllabus, is proposed in Chapter 7. The last chapter of the book treats the final stages of language program development, namely, the preparation of a proto-syllabus and the difficult question of its realization as a pedagogical syllabus, ready for the classroom teacher. Various solutions are possible; one new approach is suggested.

There has been considerable confusion, evident in the literature, over just what the functional–notional syllabus represents. It is hoped that this work will help to clarify the matter and demonstrate how a communicative approach appropriate to a particular environment and to local conditions may be prepared. Much of the work in communicative syllabus design is still very tentative, and requires a good deal of refinement. It is in this spirit that I have prepared the present volume; it is also my hope to see the area of syllabus design continue to develop, since it shows much promise for the future.

I have received a great deal of help in the last 8 years since I began working on the ideas set out here. I have had the benefit of numerous discussions with my colleagues and students both in Canada and in other countries. I would like to acknowledge particularly comments on portions of the manuscript by C. S. Jones, Lynne Young, Jane Hugo, Barbara Sandilands, D. Cooke, A. Cumming, and Barbara Mathies. Grants from both the Dean of Arts and the Dean of Graduate Studies and Research of Carleton University have assisted in the research and in the preparation of the typescript. Finally, I would like to thank my husband, Maxwell Yalden, not only for having read and commented upon the entire work, but also for his encouragement and support during its preparation.

Janice Yalden   Ottawa

Contents

Part One:

THE BACKGROUND TO SYLLABUS DESIGN

Chapter 1:

Language Teaching and Theory of Language

NORTH America in the '50s and '60s was the scene of an enormous surge of self-confidence and optimism among those working in the area of second-language teaching and learning. It subsided almost as rapidly as it had come.

The rise and fall of audio-lingual theory has been well-documented elsewhere, and it is not necessary to rehearse it here. It is as well to remember, however, that it is not only the audio-lingual method which has failed to live up to expectations. The grammar-translation method has also long been rejected for use in any situation in which the learner wants to acquire a language for contemporary, active use. And the audio-visual structuro-global method, while it has served long and well (especially in the teaching of French) has been under attack for some time.[1]*

In a word, the concept of a universally applicable method has given way to a kind of eclecticism in the classroom. The teacher is expected to proceed in accordance with 'cognitive code-learning' theory (Carroll, 1965, 1966; Chastain, 1970, 1976; Diller, 1978), choosing teaching techniques which will fit in with some broad principles of the psychology of language learning, a generalized concern for the learner's state of mind, and appropriate language learning objectives. Why not leave the issue of course design alone, then, and depend on the teacher to get on with the job? Because, simply put, this is an entirely inadequate view of the kind of training that can and should be provided for teachers.

* Superscript numbers refer to Notes at end of all Chapters.

3

This approach amounts to an admission that no one knows much about what language teaching is all about, and that there is, in fact, no guidance that can be provided for teachers who attempt to find their way through the maze of professional literature that now exists. Nor is there, in such a view, any assistance available in selecting appropriate textbooks from the large numbers available, or anything to be done when there are apparently no suitable texts in print. If no one method is universally acceptable, and if only an undifferentiated collection of teaching techniques can be provided to teachers, they are left in an uncharted land. As one teacher trainer states, in a recent *cri de coeur*:

> We may be very good in training teachers in the use of specific techniques, gadgets, in a cookbook approach to the classroom, but we have been very lax in developing a cadre of teachers who know why they do what they do... (Orem, 1981).

There are other factors as well which are bringing pressure to bear on teachers and teacher trainers everywhere. One of these is the increased awareness in society of the number of variables that must be taken into account in planning second-language teaching programs. A UNESCO working paper (UNESCO, 1975) prepared for a meeting of experts on diversification of methods and techniques for teaching second languages contains the following statement about this sort of complication:

> There is no denying that in general and in the majority of countries, the methods used for teaching a second language or foreign languages do not take sufficient account of the profound differences in the requirements and characteristics of the various groups of users, who have so little in common as regards, for example, age, learning rate and ability, motivations and interests, knowledge and mastery of their mother tongue or of other disciplines, psychological receptivity, the time which they can devote to the study of languages, the length of the course envisaged (UNESCO, 1975).

No doubt this would be an unsettling statement to present to the classroom teacher. In addition, an increased concern with the cost-effectiveness of programs confronts the teaching profession, as increasing numbers of individuals require second-language training, generally as a result of large-scale movements of population. The same UNESCO working paper also points out that language teaching didactics have failed to differentiate among teaching methods according to the objectives that learners bring with them. They list some of these objectives as follows:

...command of a written or oral means of expression, access to a literature or a culture, promotion of international understanding and of exchanges between countries, acquisition of a technical, scientific or professional vocabulary, development of the ability to analyse and synthesize knowledge through contact with other conceptual and relational structures (UNESCO, 1975).

Of course, all of these problems have been known for some time. But the solutions have been less easy to identify. The working paper cited above concludes only by indicating the need to create a new frame of reference for language teaching by drawing on linguistic studies, developmental psychology, a study of the socio-cultural context, and so on. Thus, the failure of the method concept, an increase in the number of variables to be considered, the need for cost-effectiveness and for diversified objectives all herald the urgency of finding a different approach to constructing language-teaching programs.

At the same time as the language-teaching profession has been the object of rumblings of discontent from methodologists and from society itself, theory in applied linguistics has been developing in new directions. It too suggests very strongly the need for a complete revision of traditional treatments of the second-language learner. Not so long ago, writers and researchers in applied linguistics were very much interested in the work of the structural school of linguistics and in ways to use its descriptions of the linguistic product in the preparation of better pedagogical or teaching grammars. In the '50s and '60s, application of structuralist theories produced descriptions of languages upon which teaching materials were based almost directly (Politzer, 1965). But things have changed, and today applied linguistics is vastly more complicated than it was. No matter which model is examined (Stern, 1972; Lewis, 1974; Roulet, 1975; Spolsky, 1978; Kaplan, 1980; Courchêne, 1981), it appears to consist of a number of different components—or stated in a different way, it receives input from various sources. Among these are the disciplines of psychology, sociology and educational theory.

In looking at what has been added in enlarging the concept of applied linguistics, one might begin with psychology. There is much direct interest in psycholinguistic theory and in the examination of the processes involved in second-language learning. Chomsky's work has of course been enormously influential here as elsewhere—the very notion of a generative grammar shifts attention away from the utterances themselves to the question of how it is we come to be able to produce utterances at all. This interest in process rather than in product has shown up most clearly in studies of child language, but researchers in the field of second-language acquisition have also turned to this question in increasing numbers.

Interlanguage Studies

In comparing first- and second-language acquisition studies, the largest area of overlap appears to lie in the field of interlanguage studies. Those who have developed theory in error analysis and interlanguage hold that children, in acquiring their first language, constantly engage in testing hypotheses about the nature of the language they are learning. This view derives from Chomsky's theory of a generative grammar (Chomsky, 1965, p.30), and it is argued by extension (e.g., Corder, 1967, 1978a; Richards, 1973;) that the same process occurs in the second-language learner. In the course of hypothesis-testing, learners get feedback from the linguistic environment in which they find themselves, and are thus able to correct any false hypotheses and so 'self-correct' their linguistic production. Children certainly appear to use this approach exclusively, going through a series of inter-languages, each one being a closer approximation to the adult version of the target language (whether it is their first or another). They do not seem to use any other strategy, remaining impervious to parents' attempts to correct their 'mistakes'. They seem to acquire language from mere exposure to it, resisting attempts to bring them along more quickly, and developing their proficiency in a thoroughly predictable way.

Adults, however, do not appear to possess the same ability to progress in a natural manner. Research in error analysis has pointed to the phenomenon of 'fossilization' (Selinker, 1972)—that is, to the case all too frequently encountered of the learner who repeats the same error over and over again, in spite of the fact that he 'knows' (at a conscious level) that it is an error, that his hypotheses have been proved wrong, and that his native and target languages do not always operate in the same way in particular instances. Rivers has drawn attention to the problem as follows:

The notion that repeated errors of this type can result from the learner testing the hypothesis that the two languages operate in a parallel fashion at this point (the usual explanation of the hypothesis-testing theorist) is difficult to sustain in light of the fact (frequently observed and experienced) that one is constantly repeating the same error and then immediately correcting oneself, often with a sense of mortification and exasperation at one's inability to perform according to foreign-language rules one has studied and feels one 'knows' (Rivers, 1980, p.51).

In the past, learners were subject to stern admonitions to get on with the job, cease their idleness and either study more grammar or repeat more drills. However, the phenomenon of fossilization remains extremely persistent, moral strength and good intentions notwith-standing, so much so that many researchers have attempted explanations of whether or not we in fact lose our apparently innate ability to acquire second languages as we grow older.

Neurolinguistics

Wilder Penfield's work is a classic in this regard. In one of his best known and most influential essays on this subject he complains about "school-time learning of secondary languages in the second decade of life", and gives two kinds of reasons why this is an unsatisfactory time to learn languages. There are physiological reasons: "The child's brain has a specialized capacity for learning language—a capacity that decreases with the passage of years". He goes on to say that "the brain of the child is plastic. The brain of the adult, however effective it may be in other directions, is usually inferior to that of the child as far as language is concerned" (Penfield and Roberts, 1959, p.240). He remarks that children after suffering certain kinds of brain damage will normally learn to speak again, while adults having suffered similar damage may or may not regain this ability.

Penfield also gives psychological reasons for an early start on the process of second-language learning. He speaks of the strong motivation the child has and of the fact that learning language does not form his or her primary conscious goal. From this he draws the conclusion that the impetus for learning should not be to acquire language, but to achieve success in games and problem-solving—an idea which was in advance of its time.

Penfield's statements fired interest among applied linguists—and certainly among the population at large—in neurological studies of language acquisition. A good deal of recent research has centered on the functions of the two hemispheres of the brain and on the theory of cerebral dominance. Lenneberg's widely discussed work hypothesized, for example, that the development of cerebral dominance is firmly established around puberty. He concluded that the language function is lateralized to the left hemisphere of the brain, and that "automatic acquisition [of a second language] from mere exposure ... seems to disappear after this age" (Lenneberg, 1967, p.176). This was just as discouraging a view for language teachers as that expressed by Penfield 12 years earlier.

Since the publication of Lenneberg's *Biological Foundations of Language* in 1967, there has been a large accumulation of research on the matter. It remains of fundamental importance to the understanding of the differences between the language learning and/or acquisition abilities of the adult when compared with those of the child. Puberty continues to hold its place as an important benchmark in the development of language acquisition ability, but it is not clear that the ability to acquire a second language naturally is directly related to the biological explanation alone—or even in part.

Second-Language Acquisition in Adults

Penfield's work drew attention to differences in potential between child and adult language learners. Today, there are two distinct areas of research in second-language acquisition and learning, one comprising studies in language acquisition in children, the other in adolescents and adults. In a recent commentary on the relationship between the two areas, Rivers reminds the reader that much of the second-language acquisition research carried out so far has been concerned with the process in young children in formal settings or bilingual programs. And she wisely advises caution in applying findings from first-language acquisition research to the problems that continue to surround the acquisition process in the adolescent and adult engaged in learning a second language (Rivers, 1980).

There is no question that research on adolescents and adults has been voluminous, but it has been directed primarily toward investigating the impact of various methodologies on the quality of the linguistic product, rather than toward the process of acquisition. What *is* emerging quite clearly from psycholinguistic and neurolinguistic research at this time, however, is that there are some intriguing differences in the adult's second-language acquisition process vis-a-vis that of the child, and that the differences should be given far more attention in second-language teaching than has been the case so far.

The work of Stephen Krashen is important in any consideration of psycholinguistic contributions to studies of the language-acquisition process in adults, and in designing appropriate language programs for them. While he agrees that there are differences between the child and the adult learner, his view of the adult's potential is far more positive than that of either Penfield or Lenneberg. He summarizes the current work in neurolinguistics as follows:

> While child–adult differences in second-language acquisition potential do exist, the evidence for a biological barrier to successful adult acquisition is lacking. On the contrary, there is abundant reason to maintain that adults are still able to 'acquire' language naturally to a great extent (Krashen 1981, p.81).

Krashen points out that the significance of these conclusions lies not in the expectation of any 'methodological breakthrough' in second-language instruction, but in the fact that they are consistent with current approaches to teaching, several of which have been developed pragmatically by experienced teachers, somewhat apart from theoretical considerations (Terrell, 1977; Allwright, 1978).

The approaches in question repose a good deal of trust in the ability of adolescents and adults to acquire language through means other than formal study, and emphasize activities which focus on the act of communication and the message to be communicated rather than on the linguistic means involved. Though recent research has discredited Penfield's somewhat dismal view of the inability of the adult learner to achieve anything much in second-language learning, focussing on the act of communication rather than on the means of communicating is exactly what he had suggested. It does therefore seem that interest in and the prominence given to teaching activities which center on the language-learning process is on the increase, and that this has happened with support from many areas of psychological research and from the work of practising teachers as well.

The Act of Communication

The contributions from psycholinguistic studies to applied linguistics have the effect of putting the act of communication and its place in natural second-language acquisition in the limelight. The means of communicating (i.e. linguistic forms) and formal language learning no longer take center stage. It is interesting to see how developments in psycholinguistics now can be linked to related work in sociolinguistics which has similar implications for language teaching. Rivers makes this connection when she characterizes the change of emphasis in cognitive psychology in the last two decades as being "a move from the consideration of language as an accumulation of discrete elements in associative chains to the study of human conceptual and perceptual systems and a growing interest in the pragmatics of language in situations of use" (Rivers, 1980, p.48).

Language is thus to be considered in two contexts: on the one hand, human systems of conceptualization and perception, and on the other, the actual use of language in society. Rivers points out further that this change is evident in first-language acquisition studies. Insights into semantically-based relations expressed ultimately through linguistic means have been found useful in the study of child language, and she reports that these are seen by at least one researcher (Schlesinger, 1977) to be "more descriptive of what the child is acquiring than the syntactic relations basic to the now classical form of transformational-generative grammar" (Rivers, 1980, p.49). Generative grammar (which is seen by many as belonging in the realm of cognitive psychology) was of course not initially concerned with language in use at all; quite the contrary. Chomsky stated that:

> Linguistic theory is mentalistic, since it is concerned with discovering a mental reality underlying actual behaviour. Observed use of language or hypothesized dispositions to respond, habits, and so on, may provide evidence as to the nature of this mental reality, but surely cannot constitute the actual subject matter of linguistics, if this is to be a serious discipline.... [The] serious discipline [of linguistics is] concerned primarily with an ideal speaker-listener, in a completely homo-geneous speech-community, who knows its language perfectly and is unaffected by such grammatically irrelevant conditions as memory limitations, distractions, shifts of attention and interest, and errors (random or characteristic) in applying his knowledge of the language in actual peformance (Chomsky, 1965, p.3).

Competence and Performance

Chomsky's well-known distinction between linguistic competence and linguistic performance (Chomsky, 1965), although modified subsequently, provided, in its original form, a powerful stimulus for many new theoretical developments in linguistics as well as socio-linguistic research concerned with language use, language acquisition, and second-language learning. But his limitations on the scope of linguistics have not by any means been universally accepted. In particular, the work of many British linguists is centrally concerned with language in actual use. In Halliday's work on the development of the linguistic system in the child, for example, observed use of language plays a most important part. For Halliday, language is a social activity. The child learns the mother tongue *interactionally,* in the context of learning the culture through the mother tongue (Kress, 1976, p.xxi). The fundamental question remains: how does the child do this? The *adult* linguistic system on the other hand is seen as a multiple-coding system of meaning relations, together with their realization as configurations of words and structures and the realization of these in turn as phonological patterns. It comprises content, form and expression. Thus grammar is just one part of language, and structure is just one part of grammar (Halliday, 1975, p.3).

The notion of competence and the relationship between it and performance has been very widely discussed, and the work of Dell Hymes in particular (especially Hymes, 1972) has been extremely influential in steering developments in second-language theory and practice. For Hymes, Chomsky's categories of competence and performance do not allow at all for whether what we say is appropriate to any given social context. And his statement that "there are rules of use without which the rules of grammar would be useless" made it very clear that the definition of 'competence' would have to be revised to include contextual appropriateness. Hymes also criticizes the view of performance held by the transformational-generative school, in which performance is treated as being concerned with memory and perceptual constraints, and not with social interaction at all. (Munby, 1978, in his very concise and useful discussion of the theoretical background of the present notion of 'communicative competence', calls this the 'dustbin' view of performance.) Hymes accordingly points out that applied linguistics needs a theory of language that "can deal with a heterogeneous speech community, differential competence, the constitutive role of socio-cultural features" (Hymes, 1972, p.275) and he suggests that while this may be a long time coming, the key may be provided by the notion of competence itself.

By his enlargement of the definition of competence to include the concept of communicative function, Hymes points the way to the necessary expansion of what a second-language teaching program must entail. As such, it reflects—or is reflected in—the concerns of the experts called together by UNESCO (see above) as well as the work of the Council of Europe team (see below, Chapter 4), and indeed of many other researchers in applied linguistics today:

> If an adequate theory of language users and language use is to be developed, it seems that judgements must be recognized to be in fact not of two kinds [i.e. grammaticality and acceptability] but of four. And if linguistic theory is to be integrated with theory of communication and culture, this four-fold distinction must be stated in a sufficiently generalized way ...:
> 1. Whether (and to what degree) something is formally *possible*;
> 2. Whether (and to what degree) something is *feasible* in virtue of the means of implementation available;
> 3. Whether (and to what degree) something is *appropriate* (adequate, happy, successful) in relation to a context in which it is used and evaluated;
> 4. Whether (and to what degree) something is in fact done, actually *performed*, and what its doing entails (Hymes, 1972, p.281).

Thus, for Hymes, communicative competence involves interaction among grammatical, psycholinguistic, sociocultural and probabilistic subsystems (Canale and Swain, 1980, p.16).

It is clear, then, that in recent studies in language description, as well as in psycholinguistic and in sociolinguistic research, interest has been much centered on language use as opposed to what Widdowson (1978b) calls language usage. The implications for work in applied linguistics are very considerable. In particular, Krashen's work in development of his 'Monitor Theory' has been very illuminating. While it has been referred to as no more than "an interesting, carefully elaborated metaphor of limited scope" (Rivers, 1980, p.52), since it lacks supporting empirical evidence, it does in fact contribute substantially to the discussion of the question whether language as system should include language as communicative activity. It is also important in determining whether the second-language classroom should be organized in a manner precisely opposite to current practice, by giving communicative activity precedence over formal work on the language system as such.

Monitor Theory

Krashen's 'Monitor Theory' of adult second-language acquisition hypothesizes that adults have two independent systems for developing ability in second languages, subconscious language *acquisition* and conscious language learning. So far, so good. One might indeed say that this is hardly very startling, although the fact of the matter is that the majority of the work done in our classrooms has not reflected the presence of the acquisition system at all. Teaching programs have generally been constructed as though conscious learning were the only route to mastery of a second language, either through learning 'rules', or practising the application of those rules in the production of utterances of a more or less meaningful sort in the target language. Sometimes the process has been deductive, sometimes inductive—the controversy over which was more meritorious has been the subject of debate for many years (e.g., Mackey, 1965; Yalden, 1976; Diller, 1978).

While advantages have been conceded to children who are known to be able to 'pick up' the language without formal instruction (and it has even been admitted by teachers that adults could do the same thing), it has been argued that they could be successful only to a limited degree, since without the benefit of formal instruction they would never truly master the target language. They would end up with a sort of pidginized version rather than a real command. On the other hand, one could not miss if one followed the formal approach; it might take a long time, but one would be assured of a fuller mastery, and of being able to produce 'correct' utterances, which would reflect educated usage.

The superiority of the effects of conscious language learning have seldom been subject to doubt since the eighteenth-century movement to prescriptive grammar, although before that time there were many voices raised against it. In this frame of reference, what is most surprising about Krashen's theory is not that it contains the notion that the two systems (acquisition and learning) are interrelated, but the further hypothesis that subconscious acquisition appears to be far more important than conscious learning. And the difference between the two systems lies in the fact that language acquisition is very similar to the process children use in acquiring first and second languages. It requires a kind of interaction in the target language in which speakers are concerned primarily with the messages they are conveying and understanding, rather than with the form of their utterances.

Conscious language learning is thought to be helped by the presentation of explicit rules and by the correction of the errors that learners make.[2] During the process of acquisition, learners (or acquirers as Krashen calls them) do not need to have a conscious awareness of the 'rules' they possess; and they may correct their own errors on the basis of the 'feel' they have for what is and what is not a grammatically acceptable utterance in the target language. Conscious learning, it is hypothesized, is useful—indeed, available—only as a 'Monitor'. It cannot be used successfully to initiate utterances. Fluency in production in the target language is thus based on what we have acquired or 'picked up' through active communication, and 'formal' knowledge may be used only to alter our output, once initiated by the acquired system. While the Monitor may function sometimes even before the utterance is actually produced, it cannot be used to initiate utterances in fluent production in a target language.

It is important to note that Krashen does not deny that a learner can formulate utterances at a very early stage of language learning through application of the 'rules' he has been taught. He can. But his production will be severely limited and will be quite lacking in speed and spontaneity. Again, this is hardly a revolutionary announcement for the experienced classroom teacher or any individual who has tried to learn a second language in a formal setting. What is startling is to be confronted with the possibility that we might have been going at things the wrong way around, and that rather than getting the period of formal instruction over with first, and waiting for 'practice' to produce speed and spontaneity, we might have to think in terms of providing an environment in which the learner can develop his acquisition system in an unselfconscious way, and in which emphasis on the formal system of language and on development of the learning system in the individual is considerably diminished.

The Monitor Theory is, at its present stage of development, insufficient in itself to cause a complete reversal of classroom procedures that are now commonplace. However, Krashen's suggestion that subconscious language acquisition is the central means by which adults internalize second languages (and therefore that the ability to acquire language naturally does not disappear at puberty), when taken together with research results in areas such as neurolinguistics, and with other theoretical work in psycholinguistics and sociolinguistics, provides considerable support for those who wish to explore systematically and thoroughly the advantages of a quiet revolution in second-language teaching for adults.[3]

New Directions

Psycholinguistic research suggests that, in the child, learning a second language appears to be accomplished in much the same way as acquiring the first. Exposure to language data equals acquisition, and no additional mediating or modifying system operates. Later on, for reasons which have been much debated, another way of acquiring knowledge of the linguistic system becomes possible, and the individual often attempts to apply this alternative whenever he embarks on the process of acquiring a second language. I have argued that second-language teachers have paid attention almost exclusively to the second mode (what Krashen calls 'learning') and very little or no attention to the first ('acquisition'), in spite of the fact that we have no evidence that it is less effective.

A second reason for change comes from theoretical work in sociolinguistics, and a redefinition of the theory of language. A great deal more interest is now evident in the notion of communicative rather than linguistic competence, and in communicative performance as well. Adoption of this view of language implies a more complex task for the language program designer.[4]

Finally, in planning language programs there has been a switch of emphasis from 'content', which normally meant grammar and lexis, to 'objectives'. This is yet another source of input into applied linguistics, coming as it does through curriculum theory from Bloom (1956) via Valette and Disick (1977). The way in which objectives are stated in work produced in North America differs considerably from the European approach, but in both cases the objectives refer to many variables other than linguistic content, and indeed are often seen as taxonomies of something entirely different from such content (Shaw, 1977). And the needs of the individual with regard to objectives and corresponding course content have been subjected to increased scrutiny as the number of individuals requiring instruction in languages for occupational and vocational purposes, as well as for general educational ones, has increased.

It seems, then, that it is necessary to accommodate in our language teaching programs a variety of language learners with a variety of abilities, aptitudes and objectives, and that it is also necessary to take into account modifications in theoretical work in linguistics as well as the results from empirical studies in relevant areas. These aims will have to be reached through something more sophisticated than the concept of a 'method' or a collection of teaching techniques unconnected in any particular way save the teacher's familiarity with them. There are now so many factors that need to be considered in teaching language as well as language usage that they cannot be handled in a satisfactory way within the conceptual framework that any one 'method' provides. A solution to the problem is to be found in syllabus design theory, which has arrived at an advanced stage of elaboration as a result of work in applied linguistics since the mid '60s. It is to this aspect of the matter that I now wish to turn (Chapter 2).

Notes

1. One has only to turn the pages of those volumes of *The Modern Language Journal* published in the '60s and early '70s for the chronicle of audio-lingualism in the United States, but the reader may wish to read especially Chastain and Woerdehoff (1968) and Chastain (1970). Rivers (1964) and Carroll (1966) are also particularly interesting in this regard. Bibeau (1976) and Guillo and Creus (1977) both comment negatively on audio visual methodology.
2. See Krashen (1981) for a full account of his Monitor Theory and of the research results in various relevant areas.
3. Research in bilingual education, especially the Canadian experience with late immersion programs as well as with courses taught through a second language, also strengthens the case. It is of interest particularly with regard to the design of a syllabus at the secondary level of education. See especially Allen (1980).
4. Morrow (1977) proposes seven features of communication, for example. In Chapter 6, I will put forward a number of skills which may require attention in designing a balanced communicative syllabus, as well as some indications of how they can all be 'tracked'.

Chapter 2:

The Evolution of Syllabus Design

DESPITE discussion and experimentation for more than three decades, the language-teaching profession has reached no conclusion as to which 'method' is intrinsically 'best' and it now seems unlikely ever to do so. Yet teaching materials are available in huge numbers, and have to be assessed somehow if one is to get on with the business of preparing a course and teaching one's students. It is therefore surprising that more attention has not been devoted to the question of syllabus development in second-language teaching in North America.

This may be due to a view of language learning as mastery of the 'four skills' or to the resulting difficulty of specifying objectives in any terms other than those of linguistic content. In any case, teachers of English as a second language are on the whole still more used to thinking about methodology than about syllabus design. Most practicing teachers have participated over and over in discussions concerning matters such as the use of pattern practice drills, whether or not to admit translation as a teaching device, or at what point the study of the passive voice should be introduced. But teachers are generally unprepared to produce an overall and comprehensive plan or design for a second-language course.

The problem is complicated further since pressures on language teachers and language planners to produce more efficient courses have increased greatly in the post-war world. The educational base has broadened, and there have been large population shifts both as a result of conflict and of cooperation. At the same time, theories of language and of second-language acquisition have evolved, and in spite of past hesitations over methods we do not have to feel that we are in a cul-de-sac. New perspectives on the issues involved in designing language programs have brought into sharper focus a model better suited to the task. Rather than sticking to the kind of procedure which involves an ordered progression from 'approach' to 'method' to teaching 'technique' (Anthony, 1972), it is possible to think in terms of syllabus design.

Syllabus and Curriculum

The notion of a syllabus is of course not at all new in the context of education. Ministries of education regularly produce descriptions of overall curricula to be followed in schools of all sorts, according to prevailing theories of education. Such descriptions are turned into a list of courses to be taught, and for each course or series of courses, a syllabus is provided.

While neglected in the past, syllabus design in all second- or foreign-language teaching now must take on fundamental importance. This is so since communicative language competence is viewed as consisting of a wide range of skills, of which the manipulation of linguistic forms is only one. Nevertheless, it is not an easy task to find a definition of 'syllabus' in current literature.

In North America at least, it is often used interchangeably with 'curriculum', if in fact it is used at all.[1] But for the purposes of the present discussion, I want to preserve the distinction between 'syllabus' and 'curriculum', especially as I will be referring later to the place of language studies 'across the curriculum'.

The most suitable and clear definition of the two terms is provided in A. M. Shaw's survey of the literature on second-language syllabus development (Shaw, 1977). He quotes Robertson (1971, p.564) as follows: ". . . the curriculum includes the goals, objectives, content, processes, resources, and means of evaluation of all the learning experiences planned for pupils both in and out of the school and community through classroom instruction and related programs. . ." He then defines 'syllabus' as "a statement of the plan for any part of the curriculum, excluding the element of curriculum evaluation itself". And he concludes that "the syllabus should be viewed in the context of an ongoing curriculum development process". This distinction is particularly useful if one considers that it is often necessary to give language courses which are not part of a curriculum at all. Especially in ESL such courses are a commonplace, so that a syllabus which will define a language course for a group of learners meeting entirely outside a school setting is a very useful tool.

A syllabus has been compared to a blueprint: it is a plan which the teacher converts into a reality of classroom interaction. But a syllabus can be altered with somewhat more ease than a blueprint if it turns out to be imperfect in any way. This needs to be clearly understood, lest it be thought that yet another rigid approach to language teaching is being recommended here. There is plenty of latitude for the teacher to take into account alterations in the classroom situation and respond to them, and still work within the framework provided by the syllabus designers. Some writers draw a further distinction between the 'proto-syllabus' and the 'pedagogical syllabus' (e.g. Alexander, 1979) the former being a specification of content derived from a description of the purposes the learners have for acquiring the target language, the latter representing a plan to implement the former at the classroom level. It is my belief that the term 'syllabus' must subsume both these meanings, and that it should also include an approach to testing.

The Traditional Syllabus

Until quite recently, in language teaching, one generally accepted syllabus type has dominated the preparation of teaching materials. This syllabus has generally consisted of two components: a list of linguistic structures (the 'grammar' to be taught) and a list of words (the lexicon to be taught). Often the items in each list are arranged in order showing which are to be taught in the first course, which in the second, and so on. The criteria for sequencing are various; the point is that the items *are* sequenced and the teacher regards certain points in the sequences as representing levels (e.g., beginning, intermediate, advanced; or Grades 9, 10, 11 . . .) to be reached by the students.

This kind of approach to language course design is the one tradition-ally adopted in our educational institutions, to some extent in volunteer teaching, and also in commercially operated language schools. In the last decade or so, however, this manner of setting about the task of course planning has come to be regarded as deficient, and this deficiency has been reflected in the sterile debate over method referred to above. Yet it was not fully recognized until relatively recently that no matter which 'method' was selected, any syllabus that was produced was essentially based on the same model: the selection and sequencing of linguistic structures only, the underlying assumption being that learning a language meant learning to master its grammatical system (however this might be defined). In addition, it was expected that students would acquire a reasonably adequate 'basic' vocabulary of a standard sort, again no matter which method was employed.

The acknowledgement of this difficulty in the second-language learning and teaching process coincides with profound changes in the development of linguistic theory, some of which were discussed in Chapter 1. These changes in theory of language have made it difficult at times to identify the point of merger between the interests of the theoretical linguist on the one hand, and those of the applied linguist and language teacher on the other.[2] However, a new form of alliance is becoming clear. Widdowson describes it as follows:

> It seems to me that a revolution is taking place in linguistics against a conceptual order which derives from de Saussure, and which, indeed, served as the very foundation of modern linguistics. There is an increasing recognition of the need to pay as much attention to the rules of use, the speaker's communicative competence, as to rules of grammar, his grammatical competence, and that an adequate linguistic description must account for both (Widdowson 1979a, p.12).

In general linguistics, as in applied work, the concerns are now the same. In speaking of rules of use in the latter area, we mean that what has been missing from our language programs is a consideration of how we use language in everyday situations of all sorts. When we speak our own language, or any other that we know well, we concern ourselves with much more than linguistic accuracy as we go about our business. We also make sure that we express ourselves in an appropriate fashion as we move from one context to another, and even as we function within any one context or situation. It is this quality of appropriateness that has been neglected in our teaching, and current debate and research in the area of language course design is now much centered on the question of how to introduce opportunities for and training in language use (as opposed to language usage) into the teaching process.

Synthetic and Analytic Strategies

Such a change in attitude produces a different model for the language teaching syllabus, a model which is much more complex than the one now commonly in use. A good point of departure in looking at some new approaches to syllabus design is to turn to developments in Europe. The coming into existence of the European Community triggered the production of an important and influential set of proposals for a 'unit/credit' system of language teaching for adults (Trim, 1973, van Ek, 1973). These proposals were drawn up for the Council of Europe by a team of experts from a number of countries, including several from Great Britain, and deal in the first instance with the teaching of English. The main thrust of the proposals was that a system should be devised to teach languages to adults who would now be moving back and forth from one country to another as 'guest workers' (rather than as immigrants), and who would require rapid training in fairly well-specified areas of their second languages for occupational purposes. In the course of tackling the problem of how appropriate teaching programs could be planned, syllabus design theory has received much attention. David Wilkins, one of the contributors to this project, argued (1976) that the numerous pedagogical strategies ('methods') in existence could be grouped into two conceptually distinct types of approach, labelled 'synthetic' and 'analytic', and that any actual course or syllabus could be placed somewhere on a continuum between the two.

Wilkins defines the first of these two strategies as follows:

> A synthetic language-teaching strategy is one in which the different parts of language are taught separately and step-by-step so that acquisition is a process of gradual accumulation of the parts until the whole structure of the language has been built up (Wilkins, 1976, p.2).

In planning courses based on this approach, the language items to be taught are ordered into a list of grammatical structures and probably a list of lexical items. The learner is exposed at any one time only to a limited sample of the target language, and the sample is carefully controlled by the teaching situation. The learner's job is thus to re-synthesize language that has been taken apart and presented to him in small pieces; this synthesis generally takes place only in the final stages of learning, at the so-called 'advanced' levels. Applications of this strategy are clearly seen in the traditional grammar-translation approach and also in the audio-lingual approach, despite the fact that they have long been considered diametrically opposed when examined according to other criteria. In the case of audio-lingual methodology, principles of behaviorist psychology have been used to justify the choice of language items; in any application of this strategy, language is viewed as a self-contained system, psychological in orientation. The teacher is concerned much more with *knowledge* of the language system than with its *use*.

The synthetic strategy produces a *structural syllabus* (also known as a grammatical syllabus), and what happens in the classroom is that the teacher, in following the syllabus, may use either a grammar-translation method or an audio-lingual one, or a combination or 'eclectic' approach. Whichever one he uses, the constraints are the same: the content of the syllabus has been determined by giving top priority to teaching the 'grammar' or 'structure' of the language.

Objectives of the Structural Syllabus

During the transitions from traditional grammar-translation methodology to audio-lingual teaching and then to cognitive code-learning theory, shifts occurred in views held by linguists and teachers of the psychological processes involved in second-language learning. At the same time there was the advent of a desire to provide more 'ordinary' and less literary models of language. Various teaching techniques were tried accordingly. But the objectives or purposes, whether in one method or another, were still stated in terms of linguistic forms. Steiner's discussion of performance objectives clarifies this point very well. She writes as follows:

> If we state that one of our course objectives is to enable a student to communicate with others, no one can seriously dispute this, but no one will know what we actually mean in terms of particulars, and we may not know ourselves. Communicate how? in writing? with gesture? in speech? fluently? somewhat? to a small extent? In actuality what we have considered an objective is a *purpose*. ...Our purposes are not served by using general verbs such as "understand, have an appreciation for, have a feeling for, know, enjoy, believe." What we need in foreign language teaching is to use specific verbs such as "to write in French, to answer orally in Spanish, to translate into written German, to read aloud, to select the correct answer for, to transpose from the present to the *passé composé*, to write negative commands, to identify the tense, to list the changes that occur, to conjugate in writing, to complete the following sentences in writing, to fill in the blanks in writing, to repeat the Spanish, to participate in a discussion in French, to restate in Italian, to spell correctly in French, to underline," etc., (Steiner, 1970, p.580).

Steiner goes on to discuss the desirability of detailed specification, and makes the distinction between purpose and objective as follows:

> A purpose states why a subject is being studied:
>
> (a) to apply grammer correctly
> (b) to gain appreciation of French literature
> (c) to be able to communicate in French.
>
> An objective states specifically what a student should be able to do under what circumstances and these activities should lead him to his purpose (Steiner, 1970, p.580).

The preparation of performance objectives represents a large step toward precision in defining the goals of a course of instruction. But the fact is that those goals are not substantially altered in themselves. They remain, in a structural syllabus, mastery of the substance and form of language—its phonology and lexicogrammatical system.

Selection and Sequencing

The selection and sequencing of items for inclusion in the structural or grammatical syllabus has been a matter of concern for a long time. It used to be that the writing of course materials proceeded intuitively. With the rise of scientific procedures in linguistics, the notions of frequency studies, studies of range, availability, familiarity and coverage were explored, and used in the development of teaching materials. As a result, in grammatical approaches to syllabus design, the linguistic components of the types of performance we desire for our students are analysed, then the units involved are isolated. They are then taught piece by piece to get back to the beginning: language as it is used in real life. Vocabulary has to be selected *and* ordered within this approach. Structures, however, are not selected, merely ordered, since all of the target-language structures must be taught sooner or later. Staging and sequencing are carried out according to criteria of simplicity, regularity, frequency and contrastive difficulty. Questions of social utility may also be considered in the construction of appropriate teaching materials, but they are not of the same order of importance.

A comparison of four textbooks for ESL which were written relatively recently shows sequencing of the linguistic content for beginning and intermediate levels (Table 1). The teaching of this content, which

TABLE 1: A Comparison of Four Examples of Sequencing Within a Structural Syllabus

Grammatical material presented	Dixson, Modern American English (Revised)	Lado, Lado English Series	Martin, Introduction to Canadian English	Finocchiaro & McCormick, Learning to Use English as a Second Language
Sounds of English (phonetic representation)	Gradual introduction (phonetic alphabet in intro.)	Gradual introductions	Teacher's manual only (for complete phonemic system)	Used for plurals only
Verb "to be"	Unit 1*	Unit 1	Unit 1	Unit 1
Personal Pronouns	1	2	2	1
Present Tense	3	5	3	3
Demonstrative Pronouns	2	7	2	2
Indefinite Article	2	4	1	2
Questions	1	1	1	1
Negatives	1	3	5	5
Possessive of Nouns	4	7	3	7
Plurals	1	3	4	2
Noun Modifiers	6	4	1	7
Prepositions Introduced	9	14	3	5
Possessive Pronouns	7	7	2	2

Interrogative Pronouns	1	8	3	1
Verb "to do"	5	6	5	8
Modals Introduced (Auxiliaries)	14	13	21	5
Verb "to have" (main verb)	6	-	11	11
Direct Objects	9	5	15	17
Indirect Objects	9	5	15	19
Imperative	16	-	12	-
Past Tense	10	9	14	2
Present Continuous	8	12	17	8
Future (to be going to)	10	13	21	7
Future	14	21	21	21
Present Perfect	17	20	27	18
Past Perfect	17	20	27	-
Adverbs	15	18	7	20
Adverbials	25	19	6	19
Comparative and Superlative Adj.	15	21	23	17
Count and Mass Nouns	19	-	20	15
Relative Pronouns	25	22	-	-
Past Continuous	19	-	-	-
Question Tags	-	-	16	-

* Each grammatical unit equals two lessons in Dixson and Lado: one lesson in the others.

is ordered in a remarkably similar fashion in each case, represents the main goal of the methods or textbooks which are based on the synthetic approach. The books analysed here are all representative of audio-lingual methodology, with variations, and all demonstrate an underlying structural conception of syllabus design. Examination of the tables of contents of many textbooks in second-language teaching will demonstrate the same orientation. The terminology may be different, representing the fact that any given text may be based on any one of several competing theories of grammar. But the basic approach or strategy is identical.

Some examples may serve to demonstrate the point. The table of contents of Dixson's *Modern American English* (1973) (Table 2) uses traditional terminology to present the linguistic content to be taught. The table of contents in Lado's *English Series,* Book I, (1970) (Table 3) shows a different theoretical bias, but only insofar as a different terminology is used to describe the linguistic content. It is true that the grammar in each unit is slightly contextualized, as evidenced by the titles of the units, but grammar takes pride of place. There is also an evident preoccupation with phonology, as might be expected from this author, one of the foremost figures in the development of audiolingual methodology. In Praninskas' *Rapid Review of English Grammar* (1975), (Table 4), destined for more advanced learners, the terminology is more reminiscent of Chomsky than of Fries. There are no situations referred to, and phonology is relegated to the appendices, but the basic structural orientation to the selection of content is still very obvious.

Shortcomings of the Structural Syllabus

The structural syllabus is one which is very familiar to language teachers, and which has served generations of teachers and learners alike. However, it has its shortcomings. In teaching approaches based on it, form and meaning are assumed to be in a one-to-one relation, and meaning is to be learned together with particular grammatical forms. Meaning (other than purely lexical meaning) is thought to be self-evident, and is not taught as such. Yet in the grammatical syllabus, even when we have described the grammatical and lexical meaning of a sentence, we still have not accounted for the way in which it is used in an utterance, and still less in an exchange of utterances between two or more speakers.

TABLE 2. *The Table of Contents from Modern American English (Dixson, 1973)*

What exactly is missing from second-language teaching, then, and what approach is likely to be able to supply to the learner awareness of the meanings we convey when we use language in a social context? Meaning has been taught, of course, but it has been primarily the meaning of words and sentences as isolates, and not their meaning within stretches of discourse. This is not surprising and certainly not reprehensible. It derives from how language is conceived—what kind of object one thinks it is. Brumfit expresses the changing attitude to syllabus design as follows:

> The attack on grammatical syllabuses is in part an attack on the view that language must be taught as a body of knowledge, a package, which the teacher passes to the learner. No learner is in passive possession of language; it is rather an extension of his personality, a facilitating set of abilities which is used for a whole range of unpredictable purposes (Brumfit 1980a, p.101).

In this century, the impact on second-language teaching produced by its association with structural linguistics has been considerable, starting with de Saussure's work and, in North America, continuing with the work of Sapir, Whorf, Bloomfield, Fries, Lado and their many colleagues and successors. In structural linguistics, the methodology used to describe language is very closely linked to the structuralists' conception of the object they describe. In de Saussure's theory, the entity to be described is, of course, *langue,* which is static, an abstraction, a self-contained system. It is not dissimilar to the view Lado expresses (albeit indirectly) in writing about testing the second-language learner.

> [In testing] Although initially one may favor the situation approach, a closer look should change that opinion. In the situation approach, the situations in which a language may be used and tested are potentially infinite . . . In a language approach . . . it is possible to test the entire sound system, all the major grammatical patterns, and a valid sample of the general vocabulary that the student may be expected to know . . . The situations, even if sampled adequately, do not insure coverage of the language system, while the language system will be adequate in all situations with which the student is familiar (Lado 1964, p.164).

What we expect the learner to learn is what we teach. What is taught within this view are syntagmatic relations, or the relations that exist between items present in a structure. No reference to relations which may exist between items in a structure and items that are *not* in the structure is made and so the learner is not taught anything about such relations (Kress, 1976, p.xi). The synthetic approach will thus inevitably produce a grammatical syllabus, whose goal is to lead the learners via one pedagogical strategy or another to as good a command as possible of the linguistic system of the target language.

Formal and Functional Approaches

There is another route, however, which Wilkins describes as the 'analytic approach'. Broadly speaking, within such an approach a semantic, meaning-based syllabus is produced, which leads (again via

TABLE 3. *The Table of Contents from Lado English Series Book 1, (Lado, 1971)*

Table of Contents

UNIT 1	Introductions: **This is Philip.**	1
	Affirmative Statements: **Philip is a student.**	4
	Sound of [i]: **ship**	8
UNIT 2	**Is Philip in class?**	10
	Yes/no questions with IS	12
	Sound of [iy]: **sheep**	17
UNIT 3	**I'm a student.**	19
	Forms of the verb BE: AM, ARE, IS	21
	Contrast **ship** [i] and **sheep** [iy]	26
UNIT 4	**Are you and Francis brothers?**	28
	Forms of the verb BE: YOU ARE, THEY ARE, WE ARE	30
	Personal pronouns with AM, ARE, IS	32
	Plural of nouns: **students, teachers, classes**	33
	Sound of [z]: **zip**	36
UNIT 5	**Are you Paul Martin?**	38
	Affirmative short answers with BE	39
	Sound of [s]: **sip**	43
UNIT 6	**Are you Helen Newman?**	45
	Negative statements and negative short answers with BE	47
	Contrast **zip** [z] and **sip** [s]	52
UNIT 7	**Who is he?**	54
	Information questions with BE: WHO, WHAT, WHERE, HOW	56
	Sound of [d]: **day**	62
UNIT 8	**Is John a good student?**	64
	The articles A and THE	66
	The articles A and AN	68
	Articles with singular and plural nouns	69
	Position of noun modifiers	70
	Sound of [ð]: **they**	74
UNIT 9	**Please listen.**	76
	Requests	78
	Polite requests: PLEASE	80
	Object pronouns: ME, HIM, HER, US,...	81
	Verbs with two objects: GIVE, WRITE, TELL,...	82
	Contrast **day** [d] and **they** [ð]	86
UNIT 10	**Philip speaks English.**	89
	Third person singular -S of regular verbs	91
	Sound of third person singular -S [z, s, iz]	96
UNIT 11	**Do you want milk?**	98
	Yes/no questions with DO and DOES	100
	Sound of [č]: **chin**	104

Table 3. *(continued)*

TABLE 4. *The Table of Contents from A Rapid Review of English Grammar (Praninskas, 1975)*

various pedagogical strategies) to a somewhat wider goal: that of communicative competence. The distinction that Wilkins draws between the synthetic and the analytic approach thus reflects and summarizes the theoretical considerations which impel the designer of second-language programs to re-examine his goals. The apparent conflict between the two approaches has been discussed at length elsewhere, and various attempts have been made to provide some clarification.

In a very valuable presentation of these issues, Stern (1978) distinguishes the use of the terms 'formal' and 'functional' as used in linguistics and sociolinguistics from their meanings as used in a psycholinguistic and pedagogic framework, a distinction to which I shall return later. He points out that while communicative competence comprises both formal and functional components, the same terms (formal and functional) are used to refer to pedagogical strategies. Thus one may presumably find formal and functional teaching *and* learning strategies present within a functional (or 'analytic') approach, if 'approach' is taken to mean the sum of the principles from linguistic and sociolinguistic theory which serve as the basis for language program development.

Mackey (1977) discusses the distinction between formalism in language teaching and what he calls 'contextualization'. For him, the problem lies in the earlier identification of language teaching with applied linguistics. He writes:

> In the late sixties and early seventies . . . there has been a revolt against this formalism, which had not accounted for the contextual reality of language. This reaction could be seen in the growing popularity of context-oriented audio-visual courses and the drift to the more radical solutions provided by the immersion and other forms of bilingual schooling. The theoretical foundation which was eventually placed under this movement and justified its existence became known as pragmalinguistics.
>
> Pragmalinguistics is simply a new word for an old concern. It is also known as *pragmatic linguistics, linguistic pragmatics* and, more simply, *pragmatics*. There are other names which depend on the field or doctrine referring to the phenomenon. In the field of language didactics, it has been known as contextualization (Mackey, 1977, p.1).

Canale and Swain (1980, p.2) make a somewhat different analysis:

> For our purposes it is useful to make a general distinction between *grammatical* (or grammar-based) and *communicative* (or communication-based) approaches to second-language teaching. In choosing these particular terms we hope to avoid

the confusion that has resulted from use of the more inclusive terms 'formal' and
'functional' . . . By a grammatical approach we mean one that is organized on the
basis of linguistic, or what we will call grammatical forms (i.e. phonological
forms, morphological forms, syntactic patterns, lexical items) and emphasizes the
ways in which these forms may be combined to form grammatical sentences. . .
A communicative (or functional–notional) approach on the other hand is organized
on the basis of communicative functions (e.g. apologizing, describing, inviting,
promising) that a given learner or group of learners needs to know and emphasizes
the ways in which particular grammatical forms may be used to express these
functions appropriately.

Thus we have a variety of terms, all indicating similar conceptual
poles: synthetic-analytic, formal-functional, structural-contextual,
and grammatical-communicative. I will remain within the general
framework of Wilkins' theory for the purpose of clarity in the ensuing
discussion, as his description of the dichotomy—or the two ends of the
continuum, as he sees it— is the most useful one in a discussion of
syllabus design as such. Wilkins defines analytic approaches as behavioral (not behaviorist) since they are organized in terms of the purposes
for which people are learning language and the kinds of language performance that are necessary to meet those purposes (Wilkins, 1976,
p.13). He states that within an analytic approach, it is not seen as
necessary to make a "prior analysis of the total language system into
a set of discrete pieces of language". This is so since in an approach
based primarily on meaning rather than form one relies to a far greater
extent on the learner's analytic capacities than in a structural approach.
It thus contrasts directly with the grammatical or formal approach which
relies more on the learner's ability to synthesize, or put back together,
the units of language he has learned. (An analytic approach could
therefore be related to Krashen's theories of how we use language, if
a psycholinguistic rationale were being sought. However, it may be as
well to recall that Wilkins' work, as part of the overall effort of the
Council of Europe experts, was carried out in a linguistic and sociolinguistic framework rather than a psycholinguistic and pedagogical
one.)

The Semantic Syllabus

The analytic approach leads to the production of a semantic syllabus
(See Fig. 1). However it is defined, the semantic syllabus will necessarily
be more intricate and demand more in its construction than the gram-

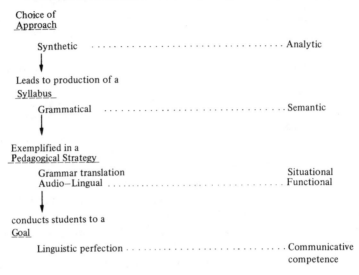

Fig. 1. (After Wilkins, 1976).

matical syllabus, since the former consists of more components. The semantic syllabus is intended to lead to communicative competence in a wide sense, rather than to linguistic competence alone; it comprises two broad types, *situational* and *notional*. Of these, the latter is more complicated to work out. The former had been fairly widely used even before the model Wilkins described had been presented through his work—it appears to run through the history of second-language teaching, turning up in the Renaissance, in the work of Erasmus and of Comenius for example. In contemporary times, it has been seen as the alternative to the grammatical syllabus (see Mackey, 1977, and Lado, 1964). Now, however, there is no general agreement on exactly where the situational syllabus belongs: while Wilkins classifies it as basically semantic, and therefore closer to the analytic approach, Canale and Swain prefer to subsume it under either the grammatical or the communicative approach, and Mackey argues that it is better classified with the grammatical or structural one. As will be shown, depending on how it is treated, it lies somewhere on the continuum from synthetic to analytic. In any case, it is certainly not an unknown quantity. The notional syllabus—or the notional–functional syllabus, as it has come to be known—is a newer concept, and therefore much less familiar.

The Situational Syllabus

The situational model is closely related to topical or thematic syllabuses (which are further examples of the semantic syllabus). All of these syllabus types have situational need as their starting point, and thus are concerned with language in a social context, as we might expect. The situational model will comprise units indicating specific situations, such as 'At the Post Office', 'Buying an Airline Ticket', or 'The Job Interview'. The topical or thematic syllabus is similar, but generally employs the procedure of grouping modules or lessons around a topic, something like barnacles clinging to the hull of a ship. One of the most popular themes in this approach is travel. One could envisage easily enough a topical syllabus on the travel theme which would comprise a series of lessons entitled 'At the Bus Station; Arriving at the Hotel; Visiting the City Hall; Going to the Science Museum', etc. The reverse is also possible: topics may be treated within a situation. For example, the situation might be 'At the Hairdresser', and the topics, 'Weather', 'Travel', 'Hobbies'.

The adoption of a situational approach has sometimes been recommended as an antidote to the drawbacks of both traditional and audio-lingual methodology. (The audio-visual method is the situational approach par excellence. *Voix et Images de France,* while not necessarily so conceived by its makers, would certainly fit into this category, as would its many offspring.) In North America, the situational approach is often realized as a wider application, or an application with a slightly different focus, of the dialogue in language teaching. Norris (1971) commented on the advantages and drawbacks of the 'dialogue' approach as follows:

> Recent attacks on audio-lingual methodology have stemmed not only from the inadequacy of its habit-theory base, but also from its apparent failure to develop competence in using manipulative skills for genuine communication. Manipulative pattern practice continues to be necessary for mastery of 'mechanical' skills in pronunciation and sentence patterns . . . but something more is needed to help the student *use* the language. The situational ('dialog') approach aimed at meaningful conversational interchange in specific contexts has suffered from haphazard

arrangement of language patterns in the dialogs which limited their effectiveness for teaching the patterns. Recent suggestions would combine the structural and situational approaches in structured dialogs, directed discourse, or situational grammar drills. 'Task oriented' exercises represent an attempt to bring students into meaningful interrelationship with each other.

It is evident from this discussion that the point of departure was not yet seen as being fully semantic. Norris still assumes at this point that sequencing means the selection and staging of 'language patterns'.

The British point of view is expressed by L. A. Hill (1967) who made a plea in the early '60s for revision of structural syllabuses along contextual lines. He wrote (p.115):

> Structural syllabuses are based on the assumption that it is enough to grade the material from a *linguistic* point of view, i.e. to look at the grading from the point of view of the structures and words to be taught. A purely contextually graded syllabus would approach the problem from a radically different point of view, i.e. from the point of view of the situations which the pupils are to be taught to respond to. I suggest a compromise between the structural and the contextual syllabus.

He justifies his proposal with the reminder that we learn a language in order to use it to communicate with others, and argues that:

> It saves a lot of time if, while we are teaching our pupils the mechanics of the language . . . we can simultaneously train them to communicate, i.e. to respond *to* language used in contexts which are natural or which resemble natural ones; and to respond *with* language used in such contexts (Hill, 1967; p.116).

He further defines the situational approach as meaning that everything taught should be taught in a situation or context that "links the words with the things they refer to". This early definition of the approach is certainly reminiscent of descriptions of the 'direct method' and of the 'structuro-global' approach.

Later work has produced at least two very full examples of the situational approach to syllabus design that show great sophistication. One is O'Neill's textbook, *English in Situations* (1970). In it, students are presented at the beginning of each unit with a 'contextualised example' of the grammatical patterns under study. These examples are entitled 'problem situation' or 'illustrative situation'; they are followed by drills and inventions (or what in North America might be called 'creative manipulation') and by 'practice situations'. In the introduction to this work, the situations are described as representing typical instances, to put the class in a natural situation where they have to use the patterns which are being drilled.

Born (1975, p.53) provides the other developed example of the situational syllabus mentioned above. He states the principles of the thematic approach as follows:

> We view each of the language skills as being interrelated and as a continuum in the totality of the language program. Language, as a living phenomenon, must provide the student with the facility to express himself in real-life situations. A thematic approach to curriculum facilitates this premise and makes it applicable at all levels of instruction. It is our conviction that the student, at every moment of his language career, must be involved in situations and activities which constantly demonstrate to him his acquired proficiency in the language.

A sample unit that 'creates the learning environment of shopping' is elaborated according to these principles. The development of language skills in the context of the environment of shopping in French, in Spanish, in German or in Italian is the main focus. The emphasis is very much on cultural differences, both cognitive and affective. The authors express the content of the syllabus as follows:

> The development of a thematic unit requires that the following curriculum components be developed systematically—key ideas, including cultural, cross-cultural, and linguistic; listening comprehension; speaking, including pronunciation, intonation, and stress; reading; writing; vocabulary (Born, 1975, p.53).

One of the objects of such a curriculum is "to increase the number of situations in which the student can perform actively in the foreign ambience", as well as enhancing "the student's ability to use the four basic skills in the foreign language". In the unit for French, there is quite specific designation of the desirability of teaching language in terms of its communicative functions. Although they are referred to as 'oral stimuli', it is clear from the list of examples that this is what is intended ('friend's suggestion', 'salesman's greeting', 'salesman's inquiry', etc.) The whole report on the thematic units is highly elaborated and constitutes a very valuable guide to the teacher of foreign languages in the United States with its comprehensive inclusion of cultural factors, appropriate phrases and so on. Note, however, the following word of caution, almost of excuse, which is provided to the reader concerning the sequencing of grammatical forms:

> N.B. In preparing these units around a specific theme, it has been necessary at times to use some structures which would normally be taught at a later time. When you encounter these structures in the Developmental Questions, please note

that they are to be taught *in context only* and *only as needed* in the particular situation. They will be thoroughly treated at the appropriate time (Born, 1975, p.59).

While the developments I have discussed above represent a step toward greater emphasis on the semantic component of syllabus design there is still something missing in their organization, in that the situation in which we find ourselves does not in and of itself necessarily determine all of what we want or need to say. A simple example of this difficulty for the teacher who is testing teaching materials was provided to me by a colleague*, who told me that he was once trying out a situational unit in an English village, the situation being 'finding your way in an English village'. He asked an aged villager one of the standard questions, "How can I get to the post office?" expecting a reply involving instructions which would have included worded like 'right', 'left', 'straight on', and references to street names or to the buildings in the village. Instead of the expected response, she offered, "Follow the old tram lines", an utterance which he had not thought of including in his 'situation', as he had not known there were any old tram lines.

Thus, we are confronted with the somewhat confining nature of the language we can teach within a situation- or dialogue-oriented approach, if we take as our main criterion for construction of the syllabus the inclusion of only those words and structures whose use is *predictable* or *typical* in any given situational context. Mackey, referring to the "holistic audio-visual approach of structuro-globalism" condemns it as over-contextualized. He writes that:

> Under-contextualization produced utterances which were grammatically correct but unidiomatic in that they did not fit the situations in which they could be used. Over-contextualization tended to produce utterances which were idiomatic but inappropriate when used outside the context in which they were learned (Mackey, 1977, p.19).

There is always an element of the unexpected in spontaneous conversation. Making complaints, requests, seeking information, agreeing, disagreeing, are not situationally determined language functions and may be encountered in any context. We may not expect an argument at the post office, but it is not impossible. The absence of the functional component from the situational syllabus is one of the major limiting

* Jon Roberts of the Centre for Applied Language Studies at the University of Reading

factors to its capacity to meet the claims that have been made for it, in terms of preparing learners for real life situations. Note, furthermore, that we can easily 'situationalize' a grammatical syllabus, but that in so doing, we will not have resolved the problem referred to earlier, namely that of teaching words and sentences as isolates.

The Notional Syllabus

The notional syllabus represents a model in which the difficulties of both grammatical and situational syllabuses are avoided. It is not without flaws, but it is an alternative which has received a great deal of attention since the early seventies, and which has had a strong impact on thinking in applied linguistics and on the work of language program designers in Europe. In its transatlantic version, it is being adapted in Canada to all levels in education. At the time of writing, it appears to be used in the United States chiefly in courses for vocational or occupational purposes, but has certainly been discussed among professionals. Its roots lie in another way of looking at kinds of meanings which have to be considered in second-language teaching.

De Saussure discussed meaning of this sort when he wrote about the category of paradigmatic relations, or relations between an item present in a structure and other items that are not so present. This view is contained in certain theories about the nature of language which have a different orientation from those of structural theories in general. Within them, a central belief is that the meaning of an utterance derives from the whole situation in which language is used, and not from words or sentences in isolation. It follows then that meaning must be approached through the study of language in use, language in discourse (Wilkins, 1976). To approach language in this way leads us directly to the study of the communicative functions of language and their relation to grammatical forms.

As an example of these relations, Allen (1977) gives a clear explanation of how the same language function interrelating with grammatical form and context can produce different realizations in any given instance. Figure 2 demonstrates plainly that there is no one-to-one correspondence between function and form. Looking at the matter from the opposite angle, one will find that in a grammatical syllabus, items such as the sentences in Fig. 3 might all be listed as examples of

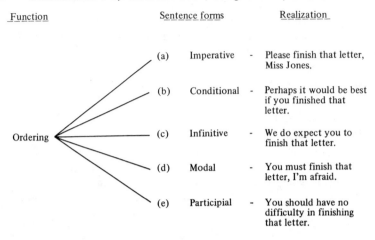

Fig. 2. Function to Form (Allen, 1977).

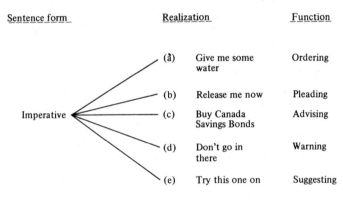

Fig. 3. Form to Function.

the imperative form. The conclusion to be drawn from these illustrations is that just as one function may be realized through several sentence forms, so one grammatical form may give rise to various sentence forms, which, while they all exemplify the same structure, do not all serve the same function.

Confronted with this situation, all speakers of any language (when they are in the receptive role of hearer or reader) have to discover the meaning that the speaker or writer intends to convey in any particular utterance. Reliance on recognition of grammatical form does not alone provide the answer. When he assumes the active role of speaker or writer, the individual has to choose something that is appropriate to the context, and which will serve his purposes at the time of utterance. It is this sort of skill together with the ability to manipulate linguistic forms we may now refer to as 'communicative competence'; it thus represents something far more sophisticated than just using gestures to order a cup of coffee. Second-language teaching has traditionally neglected the functional aspects of language competence. Traditional grammar was interested above all in teaching the propositional sentence, hence the concentration on ideational meaning plus linguistic form; audiolingual methodology, dominated by structuralist grammar, evidently was interested above all in form. In Wilkins' analytic model of a syllabus-generating approach, all aspects of meaning must be included.

The starting point is not, as in the synthetic approach, the linguistic items to be taught. It is rather the behavioral organization in terms of the purposes for which language is being learned and the kinds of language performance (in terms of language functions) necessary for such purposes. Limitation and selection are procedures that cannot be avoided, to be sure, but they must be based on new criteria. Furthermore, reliance on the learner's capacity to analyse, not to synthesize, is essential. This shift in emphasis will have immediate and important effects on classroom control of the language. Wilkins explains:

> In analytic approaches there is no attempt at this careful linguistic control of the learning environment. Components of language are not seen as building blocks which have to be progressively accumulated. Much greater variety of linguistic structure is permitted from the beginning and the learner's task is to approximate his own linguistic behavior more and more closely to the global language (Wilkins, 1976, p.2).

Analytic approaches are based on the notion of a general competence in language, and, as we have seen, are concerned with language as context-dependent. They will draw ideas from sociolinguistics, and view language as *interpersonal* rather than as personal behavior. In short, their goal is communicative competence, as defined above, and not formal perfection in the learner.

In this somewhat altered view of the nature of the language-teaching and language-learning process, Wilkins recognizes that there are now three meaning components to be considered in preparing a syllabus. These are shown in Fig. 4. It is a matter, therefore, of notions (the semantic component), functions (the interactional aspect) and structure (grammatical knowledge). (To these three components may now be added others, which include discourse and strategic skills—but these components represent a later addition to the model, and will be discussed below in Chapter 4.) In such a discussion, matters of method and presentation are not an issue. The question whether grammar should be presented explicitly or implicitly, whether a deductive or an inductive approach is better, whether we should use grammatical paradigms or dialogues, is not at all central. The selection and sequencing of the content of the syllabus is, however, vitally important.

Only after the process of ordering the content is carried out is it possible to think in terms of the presentation of the material in the classroom; and at this point, of course, 'methods' or methodology returns to the forefront of the discussion. It should be noted that objectives will also have to be stated in new terms. There will be no 'levels' defined in terms of items of the target language.[3] Levels of

Possible Components of a Syllabus

1.	The Semantic: basic concepts what to communicate	NOTIONS

2.	The Functional: Interactional aspect why we communicate	FUNCTIONS

3.	The Formal: 'grammatical' knowledge how we communicate	STRUCTURE

Fig. 4. (After Wilkins, 1976).

proficiency will be stated rather in terms of the degree of capacity of the learner to perform certain tasks. Here is an example of Level C in Listening and Speaking as defined in the *Stages of Attainment Scale and Test Battery:*

> CAN learn from a step-by step demonstration how to do something or how something works. Can ask and answer simple questions to check understanding. BUT cannot follow where there is no visual element in the illustration (ELTDU, 1976, p.13).

Alternatively, target levels may be specified as outlined in Munby (1978), in terms of such communicative features as size and complexity of utterance or text, range and delicacy in control of forms, functions and micro-skills, and speed and flexibility of communication. The central feature of a test system will be to confront the testee with a communicative task (B. Carroll, 1980, p.31), since his language performance will now be assessed in terms of communicative competence.

The notional syllabus, together with whatever methodology is used to implement it, and together also with a corresponding testing system, rests upon the belief that what we mean when we speak or write—or interpret speech or writing—depends upon the context. This "context of situation", as Firth calls it, in turn depends upon the society in which our speech act takes place. Language is seen, therefore, as essentially a function of society, serving an interpersonal role, and making each speaker a member of a speech community through its use.

Notes

1. An example is to be found in a recent issue of the *ESP Newsletter* (No. 34, January 1980). A writer comments that "Rea considers several variables which effect [sic] curriculum design", concluding that the "learner is the principal variable in course design".
2. It is interesting to note that Mackey believes that "making pragmatics part of linguistics . . . neutralized the distinction between pure and applied linguistics". He explains this as follows: "In as much as it has to do with the users and uses of language, 'applied linguistics' is . . . redundant as a separate discipline. For, pragmatically, there can be no distinction between 'applied' and 'pure' linguistics, since the theoretical problems of a language are inseparable from its real problems". (Mackey, 1977, p.12).
3. An example of this sort of specification of skills in speaking for the end of a first course in ESL, college preparatory might be: "converses hesitantly in familiar social situations but with limited control of structure and pronunciation; vocabulary is very restricted". (From a mimeographed draft of an early syllabus in English for Academic Purposes at Carleton University, Ottawa.)

Chapter 3:

Context and Function: The Roots of Change

PRIOR to the development of the notional syllabus, European writers had produced a large body of theoretical and practical work based primarily on the study of the social functions of language. An examination of these currents of thought is essential in order to situate functional views of language teaching in the context of contemporary North American theory of language and of second-language acquisition. There is of course no absolute dichotomy between North American and European developments in applied linguistics; there have been significant contributions to psycholinguistic theory from the European side (Corder's work on interlanguage is an outstanding example), as there have been contributions to the study of the functions of language in society from the American side of the Atlantic. But it will nevertheless be worthwhile to set down and clarify the ways in which differing views of what it is to know a second language can produce different emphases in theoretical studies and in their applications to language program design.

Changing Views of Language Learning

The primary preoccupation of the syllabus designer must be to decide what components will be included in a given syllabus, and in what proportion or with what emphasis. Decisions of this sort are generally made on the basis of a theory of what it is to know a second language. Broadly speaking, depending upon whether one's interest lies primarily in descriptive linguistics, in psycholinguistics or in sociolinguistics, knowing a second language might be seen in any one of these ways:

(i)   as acquiring a body of linguistic knowledge;
(ii) as acquiring a new set of habits or changing linguistic behavior;
(iii) as being able to interact in a social situation in an effective way (Corder, 1978b).

These three views of language competence in turn reflect a focus on language teaching as imparting linguistic knowledge, or as modifying linguistic behavior, or as facilitating the ability to interact socially. In each case, the functions that language serves are seen somewhat differently; but in the first two the approach to teaching is essentially formal or structural.

Until the early part of this century, language teaching was identified largely with the first view and efforts were directed primarily toward imparting a body of linguistic knowledge. Subsequently, language teaching in North America was connected in turn with phonetics (the oral approach), association psychology (direct method), and structural linguistics (contrastive analysis and audio-lingual teaching). In the '40s and '50s especially, language teaching was identified with 'applied linguistics' (Mackey, 1977). In all of these modifications, interest shifted from teaching students linguistic forms to teaching them how to change their verbal behavior (the second of the three views of language). But in the late '60s and the '70s, there was a reaction against the formalism of teaching language no matter whether it was seen as a corpus of knowledge or as a set of new habits. Instead conceptions of both language learning and language teaching were being revised once more as a result of new psycholinguistic theories. Chomsky's rejection of the behaviorist model as being inadequate to account for the complexity of human language and the creativity of the users of language marked the turning-point. His definition of the creative use of language as the ability to produce and understand an infinite number of sentences, none of which had ever been uttered before, has subsequently been criticized on the grounds that it focusses exclusively on rearrangements of the grammatical, lexical or phonological components of utterances and does not recognize the importance of "novel concatenation of non-novel meaning components" (Hasan, 1971, cited in Munby, 1978).

However, it is of more importance in a discussion of syllabus design to recognize that, because Skinnerian theory refused to consider anything that was not observable, it was unable to handle the notion of two levels of language, one underlying the other (Munby, 1978), one directly observable, the other not. This understanding of language has now become generally accepted, thus correcting the structuralist tendency to concern itself only with linguistic *product* (even to the exclusion of the component of meaning) and focussing the attention of language teachers on the *process* of acquiring a language. Chomsky, however, insists that the knowledge acquired is linguistic competence, and he excludes linguistic performance from the field of linguistic study.

The impact of transformational-generative theory on language teaching has been considerable, but in a far less direct way than the influence that structural theory brought to bear. While there were at one time exhortations to materials writers to apply transformational-generative grammar to the production of 'better' pedagogical grammars, and while attempts in this direction have certainly been made, transformational-generative theory has brought about a more evident shift from interest in the process of teaching to interest in the process of learning or acquiring a second language. With the abandonment of formalism came new efforts to find a better way; Carroll's work in educational psychology applied to second-language teaching and the evaluation of second-language programs certainly played a considerable role in sounding the knell for audio-lingual theory, and ushering in an approach to which he gave the name of 'cognitive code-learning'. A relatively recent comparison (*English Teaching Forum,* October 1976) of the audio-lingual and 'cognitive' approaches illustrates the very substantial changes proposed. In Carroll's new language learning–language teaching paradigm, language is referred to as "a highly integrated system of rules, i.e., rule-governed behavior", and language learning as "basically the comprehension of the rules of the language through which the student will be able to create sentences he has never heard before". Accordingly, the goal of language teaching is defined as *"the development of linguistic competence"*, rather than the formation of linguistic habits.

The Psycholinguistic Approach to Teaching

Subsequent to this paradigm shift, a great deal of attention in North American education has been devoted to the question of how the learner acquires or learns a second language, and how to help him develop the desired linguistic competence. Earl Stevick represents perhaps most clearly the anti-formalist approach to language teaching which has developed in North America. It is evident in his writings that knowing a second language is seen neither as acquiring a body of linguistic knowledge nor as acquiring a new set of habits. It belongs in the third category stated above, that is, being able to interact effectively with others. However, what this view has in common with the second category (changing linguistic behavior) is that learning a language is seen as being primarily a *psychological* problem, and the job of the teacher is to turn the learner into a second-language speaker, not to transmit knowledge about the system of the target language. Stevick stated in 1971 that for him language study was a "total human experience", not just an oral–aural or cognitive one: he expands this view as follows:

> Because language is ours alone, and language learning is a doubly unique experience, we often talk about it as though it were carried out by minds without bodies. The later chapters of this book will emphasize the ways in which language learning depends on the deeper reaches of the personalities of all those who are involved in the process—on their emotions and their symbolic lives (Stevick, 1971, p.3).

Stevick's work has made great strides in redirecting the attention of language-course planners and teachers to the necessity of taking into account other than purely formal aspects of what it means to know a language. The effect of his work and others such as Moskowitz, Asher, Curran and Gattegno has been to reinject meaning into the classroom, to stop the use of repetition and memorization as the sole techniques at the disposal of the language teacher, and to revive a concern for the use of language by the learner in a more communicative way.

Stevick quite rightly points out that though a student may repeat over and over the forms of language, he cannot be said to be *using* the language. This is because language use requires communication, and for Stevick communication means the resolution of uncertainties. He goes on to illustrate this view with the following quotation from Coles' *The Middle Americans:*

> We don't really follow the news that closely. I'll be doing my work, changing Paul junior's diapers or washing the dishes and I'll hear the news, but when the music comes back, I'll suddenly realize that I've been listening to five minutes, five

minutes of the news and I haven't heard a single word the man spoke, not a word. If you ask me what he said, I'd have to say nothing, nothing I can remember (Stevick, 1971, p.33).

Stevick declares that nothing was communicated to Paul junior's mother since, in the situation described, no uncertainties were being resolved and no unanswered questions were being responded to. He goes on to criticize a limitation of the view of communication which assumes that what is communicated is "facts", and he develops the argument that the "narrow-band cognitivists" both failed to realize that what matters in communication is the dimension of "depth". All normal use of language takes place at certain very deep levels of our personalities connected with "our plans, with our most important memories, and with our needs" (p.36). The *personal significance* of what is being communicated is thus of prime importance if communication is to take place. Moskowitz too refers to the importance of 'personalizing' instruction through the use of 'humanistic' techniques, and states that with these techniques the personalizing is at a deeper level than with conventional drills and exercises (Moskowitz, 1978, p.26).

'Meaning' in the Stevick triad is not the usual lexical or linguistic kind. It is used rather to refer to "what difference participation in a given activity—drill, dialogue or Spanish Club picnic—makes to an individual, relative to his or her entire range of drives and needs" (1971, p.47). It follows from this analysis that one may expect a very strong bias in favor of the psychological aspects of language learning and language teaching in Stevick's work. It is clearly his intention to draw attention to the emotional and affective states of the individual who is undergoing the process of learning a second language. He discusses drills and exercises in the framework of Transactional Analysis, within which the concept of 'ego states' is of great importance. He discusses how this framework may be used to understand the meaning of drills and exercises in classroom work, and how maintaining a proper balance among the three ego states (Parent, Adult, Child) is essential. The role of the teacher (who also has affective states) is to pull the class together into a kind of community, in which all members must depend on one another in order to get ahead. As realities are experienced individually and shared, learning becomes more profound for students and teachers alike. Stevick's general conclusion is that the learning environment must therefore be structured so as to provide for receptive, rather than defensive learning.

Of course, none of this is limited to the learning of language. It reflects current educational theory and is applied across the curriculum. But applied to language teaching, it fits neatly within the notion of two levels of language and produces a new version of what is involved in acquiring a second language. In Stevick's words, "The crucial factor in second-language learning is the quality of personal activation", a view which he contrasts with earlier interest in either the quantity of oral activity (in the audio-lingual approach) or the quality of mental understanding (in traditional or cognitive approaches).

Much of the empirical research carried out in North America in recent years reflects a similar preoccupation with language learning or acquisition as a psychological problem. It is argued by several authors (for example in Oller and Richards' 1973 collection, *Focus on the Learner*) that neither transformational nor structural grammar in second-language teaching gives sufficient attention to the use of language to convey information, and that the ability to code both linguistic and extralinguistic information through language is essential to an adequate theory of second-language learning. Oller himself argues that sentences have meaning *because* they are used in communication and points to pragmatics as being able to provide some of the answers needed in language teaching (Oller, 1973, p.37).

What is striking in all of the above is the degree of concern with the psychology of the individual who is engaged in the process of acquiring a second language, and the minute observations which are made of his performance along the way. One has only to think of the large number of studies in error analysis and learners' language to be aware of the change. Contemporary work in psycholinguistics has added a personal, performance-oriented dimension to both language-learning and language-teaching theory and data gathered on the performance of learners (i.e. their interlanguage states) are accepted as a valid object of linguistic study. To some extent, we have arrived at the third view of language learning expressed at the beginning of this chapter.

The Learner as Social Being

Through the centrality of concern with the process the individual undergoes in learning a second language, interest has emerged in the concept of communicative competence and communicative language teaching. This new vocabulary has thus far been applied primarily in North America in the context of psycholinguistic studies of the individual and humanistic teaching techniques designed to take into account newer theories of learning. But it is possible to take instead as a point of departure the premise that language is primarily a *social* function and should therefore be studied as a *social* phenomenon.

From this vantage point, one would be interested in what it means to become a *user* of a second language, rather than in the psychology of the second-language speaker on how to acquire a second-language system. These are all different theoretical perspectives (Corder, 1978b), and will produce different approaches to language teaching. Interest in the learner as a member of society and in the social functions of language has long been apparent in European linguistics. It has produced a distinctive view of communicative language teaching, which differs at many points from the prevailing North American one. The two views complement one another, however, and when studied together, provide a sound basis for a fresh start in language program design and the production of a different kind of syllabus for general as well as specific purposes. It is therefore important to trace the emergence of the European perspective if one is to clarify European–North American differences and to show how the two approaches may be integrated and exploited in a communicative syllabus design.

Linguistics in Europe has never excluded from consideration the relationship between language and the context of its use. Long before the emergence of linguistics as a separate discipline, philosophers had of course studied the question, but in more recent times, anthropologists and sociologists as well as linguists have produced theories concerning the link between speech and its context.[1] From the early years of the century, each of these disciplines has come at the same problems of thought, language and meaning from its own vantage point, and the researcher in linguistics or the teacher cannot expect to be aware of developments in his own discipline without some knowledge of the others. In particular, in order to understand the premises on which notional–functional and communicative syllabus design are based, it is necessary to know something both about these cross-discipline currents and the history of the functional or contextual view of language. A convenient starting-point is the publication, in 1916, of de Saussure's *Cours de linguistique generale,* the inauguration, in Robins' phrase (Robins, 1967), of twentieth-century linguistics.

The History of the Functional View

Of de Saussure's many contributions, the one of most interest here is his distinction between *langue* and *parole.* While he insisted that *langue* was the proper object of study of scientific linguistics, he recognized that it was implanted in each individual by his upbringing in society, and that the basic elements of each language constantly changed value. But he was not prepared to take the context of language use into account in the elaboration of his theory, convinced as he was that *langue* was *forme.* Content analysis was to be independent of extralinguistic criteria, and only relations *between* elements—not the elements themselves—were to be the object of study. Thus, while two levels of language were distinguished, one was set aside and the problem of language use and the context of language was shelved as far as linguistics was concerned. If anything, the whole matter was considered to be related to semantics, the study of meaning, which was to be left to the philosophers.

All of which is not surprising, since philosophy has been grappling with the problem of meaning and communication since Plato and Aristotle. Locke, Mill, and Kant are names that come at once to mind as being of particular interest to linguists or Ogden and Richards or Russell and Wittgenstein. In contemporary studies in linguistics the writings of Austin and Searle and of Grice are of direct concern, so much so that boundaries between disciplines seem blurred. Nevertheless, it is as well to remember that they do represent distinct areas of concern, albeit exercising a marked influence on one another, if we are to appreciate the interdisciplinary beginnings of the functional view of language as defined in linguistic terms.

Ogden and Richards published the first edition of their philosophic work on meaning in 1923. In it appeared a supplement written by Bronislaw Malinowski, Professor of Anthropology at the University of London, who had done many years of field work on what Ogden and Richards refer to as "the peculiarly difficult border-lands of linguistics and psychology" (Ogden and Richards, 1946, p.ix).

Malinowski was writing as an ethnologist in support of Ogden and Richards' view of meaning. He describes his experience in the Trobriand Islands, and draws certain conclusions from it which are of fundamental importance to our understanding of subsequent work in linguistic theory. In discussing the fact that, in analysing primitive languages, the "meaning of any single word is to a very high degree dependent on its context", he writes:

> This latter again [the expression 'we paddle in place'] becomes only intelligible when it is placed in its *context of situation,* if I may be allowed to coin an expression which indicates on the one hand that the conception of *context* has to be broadened and on the other that the *situation* in which words are uttered can never be passed over as irrelevant to the linguistic expression (Malinowski in Ogden and Richards, 1946, p.306).

Lest anyone think this is true only of primitive languages, Malinowski expands his argument and states that this widened conception of *context of situation* makes clear the difference in scope and method between the linguistics of dead and living languages, a statement of some importance at the time when the difference between the diachronic and synchronic views were just emerging.

Malinowski distinguishes between dead languages which survive only in inscriptions, modern civilized languages, "of which we think mostly in terms of written records", and "a primitive tongue, never used in writing, where all the material lives only in winged words, passing from man to man". He says that in the former cases "the meaning is wholly contained in or carried by the [inscription or] book". With the printed text before him, "the reader, at the writer's bidding, undergoes a series of processes—he reasons, reflects, remembers, imagines". But in real life, a statement "is never detached from the situation in which it is uttered . . . In each case, therefore, utterance and situation are bound up inextricably with each other and the context of situation is indispensable for the understanding of the words". Malinowski goes on to claim that the ethnographer's perspective is the real one for the formulation of valid linguistic conceptions, and that of the philologist fictitious and irrelevant. "For language in its origins has been merely the free, spoken *sum total* of utterances such as we find now in a savage tongue". Therefore, he continues, " . . . the meaning of a word must always be gathered, not from a passive contemplation of this word, but from an analysis of its functions, with reference to the given culture" (p.309).

He concludes that his analysis of meaning in primitive languages provides confirmation of Ogden and Richards' theories, since the realization of the connection between linguistic interpretation and the analysis of the culture to which the language belongs shows that neither a word nor its meaning has an independent existence. For Malinowski's analysis then, de Saussure's exclusion of extra-linguistic criteria is unacceptable. Equally important, in its primitive uses, language is "a mode of action, not an instrument of reflection" (p.312). This is so even for narrative forms, since, to use Ogden and Richards' terminology, the referential function of a narrative is subordinate to its social and emotive function.

In Malinowski's work are thus to be found two important concepts: the context of situation as indispensable for understanding language; and the subordination of the referential to social and emotive functions. The notion of language as primarily a mode of action, constituting a mode of thought only in certain societies and forms, is also fundamental. In it can be perceived the germ of the functional–notional approach, in which sociolinguistic studies take on such great significance, in which language equals communication, the creation of discourse, meaning. (This is in fact Corder's definition of language given in a paper delivered in Montreal in 1978.)

Pragmatic Theory

Malinowski was not alone, of course, in his interest in context. In the United States, a similar concern with context in the unravelling of meaning may be discerned. C. S. Peirce, the logician, writing in 1908, stated that he had come to realize that those who devoted themselves to discussing "the general reference of symbols to their objects would be obliged to make researches into the references to their interpretants, too, as well as into other characters of symbols, and not of symbols alone but of all sorts of signs" (cited in Ogden and Richards, 1946, p.279). Although as Ogden and Richards point out "his terminology was so formidable that few have been willing to devote time to its mastery", it was from Peirce that William James borrowed the idea and the term *pragmatism* (or pragmaticism, as Peirce wrote), which today turns up in Oller's pragmatic theory of language (Oller, 1971).[2]

In presenting this theory as an alternative to Chomsky's, Oller defines pragmatics as:

> . . . the study of the correspondence of linguistic forms to contexts. It logically includes syntax and semantics . . . pragmatic factors appear to be more important than phonological and syntactic ones when it comes to matters of speech perception, production, and language learning. . . . Pragmatics places emphasis not so much on entities as on their relationships within a broader perspective. It is because of the relation which linguistic forms have to extralinguistic settings that William James spoke of the "cash-value of words". . . This value is set by the rules of usage which govern what people say in order to convey meanings. These are the rules that a child learns in acquiring language, and that the language teacher seeks to instill in his students (Oller, 1973, p.47).

In applied linguistics today we tend to consensus. We accept that in the understanding of meaning and in our attempts to communicate it context is a necessary component. To explain how language works by separating form from context, and thus from meaning, seems unprofitable, not to say impossible. Yet this is what linguists have been doing for the most part, and the notion that context belongs in the province of other disciplines and was not properly part of linguistic science has made it difficult to apply theory in either general or descriptive linguistics to the design of language-teaching programs. Now, however, this is no longer the case.

As we have seen, a theory of pragmatic linguistics is being elaborated within the North American school of applied linguistics. And concern with context has never been absent from the work from applied linguistics in Europe, though it has developed there in a primarily sociolinguistic (rather than a psycholinguistic) framework. The sociological viewpoint implies a functional view of language, one in which society rather than the individual is at the center of the picture. The social aspect of language thus becomes the reference point for the biological aspect, rather than the other way round (Halliday, 1978, p.16). Those who hold a functional view of language will be interested in what functions language serves in the life of the individual as a member of society, or what he can *do* with or through language.

It follows, then, in this account, that the linguistic means used by human beings to enter into, establish, develop and maintain relationships are of primary importance, rather than the psychology of language acquisition. Halliday's (1978, p.18) statement of the relationship between the two areas is as follows:

> More important than the grammatical shape of what the child hears, however, is the fact that it is functionally related to observable features of the situation around him. This consideration allows us to give another account of language development that is not dependent on any particular psycholinguistic theory, an account that is functional and sociological rather than structural and psychological. The two are not in competition; they are about different things.

Functional theory is thus about the social rather than the psychological processes involved in language. As such, it is concerned with language as a form of interaction, and must also be concerned with the context in which such interaction takes place. It is important to bear this in mind in the context of syllabus design, as it has sometimes been said that in developing the framework for the analytic approach, and in its realization as the functional–notional syllabus, psycholinguistic aspects of language teaching have been ignored. It is rather a question of reference point.

The Functions of Language

Once the functional view of language is adopted, it is evident that the central question becomes: what are the functions of language? And for applied linguistics the question whether some are more important or occur more frequently than others also becomes of vital importance in matters of syllabus design and language pedagogy. It is not enough to say that the main use of language is communication, a phrase which has become trite in the extreme. It is a far more intricate and subtle question, one which has received a good deal of attention recently from philosophers, ethnologists, rhetoricians, and linguists alike.

Returning to Malinowski, we find that he spoke of language as being dependent on the society in which it was used, and thus not a self-contained system at all. He noticed that language evolved so as to meet the demands of any given society, and also, that its use in that society was entirely dependent on the context. Meaning, he said, comes "not from a passive contemplation of the word, but from an analysis of its functions, with reference to the given culture". He distinguished six types of language use: 'pragmatic', 'narrative', 'ritual' (magic), 'scholastic', 'theological', and 'scientific' and suggested that the extent to which they were found in a given society depended on how highly developed their culture was. Four stages of culture (savage, barbarous, semi-civilized and civilized) were posited; and Malinowski wrote that these stages were reflected in the structural strata of any given language.

Ogden and Richards (1946, p.226–27) provide a list of five functions of language, and take the grammarians to task for so often ignoring them:

> We have discussed above the half-hearted fashion in which from time to time they [the grammarians] have admitted an affective side to their problems. But even this recognition is rarely made prominent. The five functions here enumerated—
> (i)   symbolization of reference;
> (ii) the expression of attitude to listener;
> (iii) the expression of attitude to referent;
> (iv) the promotion of effects intended;
> (v)   support of reference;
> appear to be exhaustive.

Implicit in these authors' categorization of functions is a different frame of reference from Malinowski's. The latter is interested in stages of cultural development, the former in 'the affective–volitional system' of the human being as it interacts with 'speech material'. While Ogden and Richards do not elaborate on these categories, coming as they do at the end of their work on meaning, they do provide two further observations on language functions which are important in the present discussion. First, they point out that the functions do not occur in isolation.

> Most writing or speech then which is of the mixed or rhetorical kind as opposed to the pure, or scientific, or strictly symbolic use of words, will take its form as the result of compromise. Only occasionally will a symbolization be available which, without loss of its symbolic *accuracy,* is also *suitable* (to the author's attitude to his public), *appropriate* (to his referent), *judicious* (likely to produce the desired effects) and *personal* (indicative of the stability or instability of his references). The odds are very strongly against there being many symbols able to do so much. As a consequence in most speech some of these functions are sacrificed (Ogden and Richards, 1946, p.234).

And the second observation of importance in this discussion follows at once:

> These instances of the dropping of one or more of the language functions lead us naturally to the most remarkable and most discussed case of such variation, the distinction, namely, between the prose and the poetic uses of language. In these

terms the distinction is not happily symbolized, poetry being best defined for the most general and most important purposes by relation to the state or states of mind produced by the 'poem' in suitable readers and without any relation to the precise verbal means. Instead therefore of an antithesis of prose and poetry we may substitute that of symbolic and emotive uses of language (Ogden and Richards, 1946, p.235).

Malinowski supported Ogden and Richards' interest in the psychological aspects of meaning and their general views on language as logic and as psychology: he went on, of course, to elaborate on language as social behavior, as a mode of action. In this way, Halliday's statement on the complementarity of the functional view of language to the structural one is anticipated.

The Prague School

In linguistics in the '20s and '30s, as in other disciplines, the matter of the functions of language was being looked at with some care. While the primary importance of the work of the Prague School[3] lies in phonological theory, their functional approach to language was also characteristic:

This approach visualizes language as a tool performing a number of essential functions or tasks in the community using it. The most outstanding (and most obvious) among these tasks is undoubtedly the communicative function, serving the needs and wants of the mutual understanding of individual members of the given language community (Vachek, 1972, p.14).

The Prague linguists felt that this approach enabled them to contribute significantly to the discussion of questions of language teaching, and in fact they have always been interested in the application of their linguistic theory, especially to language teaching.

Their view of language functions was given its greatest elaboration by Roman Jakobson whose distinction between everyday language and poetry was the point of departure for his functional exploration of language. Unlike Ogden and Richards, however, he separated the communicative function of both practical and emotive language from the poetic function. Later on, he modified his approach, combining it with the model of Karl Bühler, who had developed a conception of the triadic instrumental character of speech. In it, three fundamentals of the speech situation are distinguished: addresser, addressee and things as the object of discourse. The discourse, depending on which of the three dominates, will show primarily an *emotive,* a *conative* or a *referential* function (Holenstein, 1976, p.153). Jakobson filled out this model as follows:

> Language must be investigated in all the variety of its functions. Before discussing the poetic function we must define its place among the other functions of language. An outline of these functions demands a concise survey of the constitutive factors in any speech event, in any act of verbal communication. The ADDRESSER sends a MESSAGE to the ADDRESSEE. To be operative the message requires a CONTEXT referred to ("referent" in another, somewhat ambiguous, nomenclature), seizable by the addressee, and either verbal or capable of being verbalized; a CODE fully, or at least partially, common to the addresser and addressee (or in other words, to the encoder and decoder of the message); and, finally, a CONTACT, a physical channel and psychological connection between the addresser and the addressee, enabling both of them to enter and stay in communication (Jakobson, 1960, p.353).

Like Ogden and Richards, Jakobson expects the functions to overlap in verbal messages, for which he believes that a set toward the context (referential function) is often the primary one. But he states that the linguist must take into account the other functions as well. He supports this view by stating that "if we analyze language from the stand-point of the information it carries, we cannot restrict the notion of information to the cognitive aspect of language" (p.354). Jackobson's schema of the factors "inalienably involved in verbal communication" is shown below. (Holenstein, 1976).

CONTEXT
(referential)

MESSAGE
(poetic)

ADDRESSER _____ ADDRESSEE
(emotive)   (conative)

CONTACT
(phatic)

CODE
(metalingual)

Jakobson's categorization has been widely adopted, but has unfortunately led some to interpretations in which expressive ('poetic') speech is separated too radically from transactional ('communicative') speech. That this is an artifical dichotomy has been well demonstrated by Britton, in his work in the area of language development in the child (Britton, 1970). He situates the two functions on a continuum, adds the poetic one, and by analysing transcripts of actual conversations, shows that the speakers move in various directions, even though the overall tone may be expressive if the talk is among a group of friends or, on the other hand, conative-informative in a business setting.

(Participant role------------------role of Spectator)

CONATIVE

EXPRESSIVE   POETIC

INFORMATIVE

The idea of language functions has thus had an impact in mother-tongue education as well as in second language teaching, and one may expect to see more interplay in the future between the work of the rhetorician and the applied linguist.[4]

Firth and Halliday

In Britain, the development of general synchronic linguistic theory owes an enormous debt to J. B. Firth, who was the first holder of a title in linguistics in that country. He had little sympathy for what he called the 'mechanical processes' of the American linguists of the '40s and '50s, though he was their contemporary. While he was, like Bloomfield, influenced by the work of anthropologists, his work developed in quite another direction from that of the structuralists. He saw his own approach as a "combination of the theoretical and the empirical approaches" (Firth, 1968, p.43), and thought that the development of theory was more important than that of procedures or methods. He derived his theory of 'context of situation' from Malinowski, even adopting Malinowski's term; however, as contextual theory, it was bound to differ greatly from structuralism. Firthian theory is important in this attempt to trace the routes by which applied linguistics in Britain comes to the functional syllabus, because it proves to be the main doorway through which the notion of context of situation and the study of language functions subsequently entered the discussions of syllabus design.

Firth acknowledges his debt to Malinowski as being "one of the makers of linguistics as we now understand it in this country". He places Malinowski's ideas as being "truly in the tradition of British empiricism and of the philosophic radicals and utilitarians", and says that it finds echoes in Wittgenstein who wrote that the meaning of words lies in their use (Firth, 1968, p.138). He also makes frequent references to functional grammar (in particular that of Temple) and says that both Malinowski and he himself agree with some of its general principles. He quotes Malinowski as stating that "The lack of a clear and precise view of linguistic function and of the nature of Meaning has been, I believe, the cause of the relative sterility of much otherwise excellent linguistic theorizing" (Malinowski, 1923, p.471), and reminds the reader that Malinowski repeatedly drew attention to the need for an adequate theory "devised for the purpose of observation of linguistic fact". (Malinowski, 1920, p.78, cited in Firth, 1968, p.146).

Firth explicitly tells us that he himself has developed the application of 'the situation theory' (sometimes also known as the contextual theory) in descriptive linguistics (1968, p.147). Of course, Firth extended it by treating *all* linguistic description as the statement of meaning, and fitting it into a technique of linguistic rather than cultural analysis. His suggestion was that ". . . linguistics at all levels of analysis is concerned with meaningful human behavior in society", and that Malinowski's outstanding contribution was his "approach in terms of his general theory of speech functions in contexts of situation, to the problem of meaning in exotic languages and even in our own" (1968, p.161).

Malinowski and Firth both represent a view of language as context-dependent and sociological in orientation, as opposed to a more internal view in which language is a self-contained system, psychological in orientation. Both men had a strong influence on the work of Michael Halliday, who in turn has had a great impact on applied linguistics in

Britain and elsewhere, and on account of whom the whole question of meaning and context of situation remains at the forefront. His more recent writings have a strong sociolinguistic, functional bent, and in them he examines such questions as the development of language functions in the child (for example in *Learning How to Mean,* 1975), and the functions language has in society. These works are necessarily connected to his formal linguistic theory (known as systemic grammar), but this aspect of his work is of less direct interest in the framework of syllabus theory, and the following account is therefore confined for the most part to developments which have led to the design of the functional–notional syllabus.

Halliday explains the context of his work on language development in children as follows:

> It was in the language of young children that Malinowski saw most clearly the functional origins of the language system. . . . all uses of language, however abstract, and however complex the social structure with which they were associated, were to be explained in terms of very elementary functions (Kress, 1976, p.8).

But it was only as the focus of attention in such studies gradually changed from acquisition of sounds to include words (size of the child's lexicon), then to mastery of structures (child's grammar), and finally to linguistic functions (meaning), that Malinowski's theories became relevant.

> Only recently has language acquisition come to be seen as the mastery of linguistic functions, and it is this perspective that is needed here, in which learning language is learning the uses of language and the meaning potential associated with them; the structures, the words and the sounds are the realization of this meaning potential. Learning language is learning to mean (Kress, 1976, p.8).

One has to ask therefore what are the functions of language that the human being masters in order to be able to 'mean'. In the child, Halliday has found that the correspondence between functions and utterance is straightforward, one-to-one. The younger the child one observes, the more clear-cut are the functions, whereas with an approach based on structure, the opposite is true. In his study of Nigel (Halliday, 1975), he used a framework of seven initial functions:

1. *Instrumental* ('I want'): satisfying material needs.
2. *Regulatory* ('do as I tell you'): controlling the behavior of others.
3. *Interactional* ('me and you'): getting along with other people.

4. *Personal* ('here I come'): identifying and expressing the self.
5. *Heuristic* ('tell me why'): exploring the world around and inside one.
6. *Imaginative* ('let's pretend'): creating a world of one's own.
7. *Informative* ('I've got something to tell you'): communicating new information.

These are arranged in the order in which they appeared from 9 months onwards, before the child had a recognizable linguistic system. Halliday speaks of there being several meanings in each function ('function', 'intention', and 'purpose' being used more or less interchangeably) (Halliday, 1978, pp.19–20). Learning the mother tongue is interpreted as progressive mastery of a number of basic functions of language and the building up of a 'meaning potential'[5] in respect of each.

Adult language, as one might expect, is functionally far more complex than that of the child. Each adult utterance serves more than one function at a time. Furthermore, the variety of social functions is much greater. Halliday notes that while the informative or 'representational' function emerges late in the child, it comes to predominate later on. So much so that adults are surprised to be confronted with the possibility that language serves other purposes as well.

> What happens, then, in the course of maturation is a process we might call 'functional reduction' whereby the original functional diversity of the child's language—a set of fairly discrete functions, each with its own meaning potential and therefore its own grammar—is replaced by a much more highly organized and more abstract, but also much simpler, functional system. The immense functional diversity of adult language usage—immense, that is, if one simply asks 'in what activities of daily life does language play a part?'—is reduced in the internal organization of the language system to a very small set of functional components, or 'macro-functions' (Kress, 1976, p.19).

The macro-functions are three in number:

1. The *interpersonal* function: to establish, maintain and specify relations between members of societies.
2. The *ideational* function: to transmit information between members of societies.
3. The *textual* function: to provide texture, the organization of discourse as relevant to the situation.

Each of these components makes a contribution to the structure, so that a grammatical structure is a composite, as it were polyphonic pattern in which one melodic line derives from each function (Kress, 1976, p.xix).[6] Language is as it is because of what it has to do (Halliday, 1978, p.19), but the reader is cautioned not to equate 'function of language' with 'use of language'. In Halliday's view there is an indefinitely long list of 'uses' which the adult has for language, but only three (or possibly four) highly-generalized functional components.[7]

The definition of the 'social functions of language' is elaborated at various points in Halliday's writings (e.g. 1976, p.9). The important point to be made here is that the individual builds up a 'meaning potential' for each function (that is, the ability to use language in each). As Halliday defines it, the meaning potential is a network of options, the ability to manipulate some structural configurations (1976, p.7). The social functions which language serves determine the available options and their structural realizations. Halliday stated in 1976 that meaning potential was what he understood by Hymes' 'communicative competence', but that he preferred his own term, since he was interested in what the speaker can *do*, not in what he *knows*. Later on, he writes in a more emphatic tone about the differences (perhaps somewhat unfairly, as Munby, 1978, p.13, suggests).

> We could say, following Dell Hymes, that it is part of the speaker's 'communicative competence' that he knows how to distribute lexical items in a text according to different kinds of language use; but there is really no need to introduce here the artificial concept of 'competence', or 'what the speaker knows', which merely adds an extra level of psychological interpretation to what can be explained more simply in direct sociolinguistic or functional terms (Halliday, 1978, p.32).

Two Frameworks

The contrast is thus clear. There are two complementary frameworks within which to work: the psycholinguistic and the sociolinguistic. The theoretical linguist may prefer to choose one or other for the purpose of developing a general theory of language; in applied linguistics and in designing a second-language program it is necessary to take both into consideration. The learner's individuality, as well as his membership in a social group must be considered, lest we leave ourselves open to the accusation that we treat students as puppets on the one hand or as though they were to live in isolation on the other.

Potential personal as well as interpersonal outcomes of the language learning process are vital components of the design, especially in working with adults and adolescents. While Stevick's concern with depth is advisable and while humanistic pedagogy will take into account and exploit the affective states of the learner in a way that has not been attempted previously it falls short of the goals set out for the language program designer. The social uses of language are unaccounted for, and the emphasis remains entirely on the *personal;* what needs to be taken into account as well is the *interpersonal* aspect of language use. What the learner knows and feels is important, but so is what he is able to do through language.

Thus it seems that there is no escaping the notion that language serves a variety of functions. In teaching second languages today, one is very often faced with groups of learners who have fairly clearly identifiable aims in learning the target language. Even if they are not specified in advance, as in courses in English for Specific Purposes (ESP), they can be investigated and tapped as a powerful source of motivation. The most recent developments in applied linguistics in Europe and in Britain reflect the adoption of the sociolinguistic perspective as the point of departure, and the notional–functional syllabus has been the result. At the same time, North American concern with the psycholinguistic framework has yielded new insights into the process of language acquisition.

It is important that the syllabus designer be able to profit from both currents of thought, and elaborate a procedure which will take into account the best of both worlds. The task should be to adopt a reasonable description of what it is to know and use a language; to identify as far as possible the most important, frequent, powerful elements of the descriptions (given the purposes of any particular group of learners); and to consider how to allow for their pedagogical treatment in the language program. In developing the notional–functional approach to syllabus design, the primary concern in Europe was with the first two of these three procedures. It is time now to look at something of the history of this model and to examine some of the variations on the original conception which have arisen with the passage of time.

Notes

1. Currie, in writing about European syllabuses suggests that an interesting link may be traced between the postulates of notional syllabuses and the principles of traditional rhetoric. He believes that "a direct and logical route leads us from the rhetoric of the nineteenth century in Europe, particularly in Scotland, to the situational semantics of our own decade, with semantic syllabuses as the most popular focus of this". (Currie, 1975, p.349).

2. For a full discussion of the history of the term *pragmatics* and of the relevance of pragmatic philosophy to linguistics, see Mackey (1977). This author concludes that pragmatic philosophers have had a wider view of language than linguists have had, and have always taken the context of reality into account. "One could argue therefore that it is not pragmatics that is a branch of modern linguistics, but rather linguistics which is part of pragmatics" (pp.3-4).

3. The Prague school was a group of scholars, mostly Czech or Russian, which held regular meetings during the '20s and '30s and published the *Travaux du cercle linguistique de Prague*. Their activities were interrupted by World War II. Since then, the community of Czech and Slovak linguists has continued to work actively. The figures of Trubetzkoy and Jakobson are central.

4. On functions as viewed in contemporary works in mother tongue education, see Andrew Wilkinson, *Language and Education* (1975). He speaks of three kinds of 'activity' going on in any interchange involving young children: "Who am I?" (introspection) "Who are you?" (relations with others) and "Who/What is he/she/it?" (exploring). He also expects multiple functions in any given utterance. Selected papers from an initial meeting of rhetoricians and applied linguists appear in Freedman, Pringle and Yalden, *Learning to Write: First Language, Second Language,* forthcoming.

5. The term 'meaning potential' is defined by Halliday (1978, p.21) as follows:

> Language is being regarded as the encoding of a 'behaviour potential' into a 'meaning potential'; that is, as a means of expressing what the human organism 'can do', in interaction with other human organisms, by turning it into what he 'can mean'. What he can mean (the semantic system) is, in turn, encoded into what he 'can say' (the lexicogrammatical system, or grammar and vocabulary); to use our own folk-linguistic terminology, meanings are expressed in wordings. Wordings are, finally, recoded into sounds (it would be nice if we could say 'soundings') or spellings (the phonological and orthographic systems).

6. See also Kress (1976, p.24) for further discussion of the role of "What we recognize as 'grammar' . . . in the traditional sense [as being] the inter-functional hook-up . . ."

7. Halliday refers to the possibility of a fourth, a *'logical'* component (1976, p.30), but says it is not of concern to his argument. In a later work (1978, p.21) he includes expressing logical relations as one of the four basic functions.

Chapter 4:

Language Functions in Applied Linguistics

IN ALL of the early work associated with the notional syllabus, matters of pedagogy were left aside. Though this approach may seem unusual when compared with any of the 'methods' so familiar to teachers, in which methodology is an integral part of an overall approach to second-language teaching, there is nevertheless a good reason for it. The notional syllabus has been developed from a sociolinguistic viewpoint and the primary purpose of those who have worked on it has been to identify the elements of a target language which its learners, as members of a particular group and with particular social and occupational purposes in mind, would most need to know. The secondary stage (the actual implementation or delivery of the program) is not elaborated; it is left up to teachers and those responsible for concrete teaching programs to see to it that the syllabus is carried into the classroom.

The Notional–Functional Syllabus

The Starting Point of the Notional Syllabus

The starting point is fundamentally different from that of the structural syllabus. Furthermore, while the approach taken to meaning and to language functions in applied linguistics has clearly been influenced by work in other disciplines and by theoretical writings in linguistics, it has taken on a distinctive quality. In Wilkins, for example, there is stronger emphasis on Halliday's second-order component of meaning potential (what the learner can mean) than on his macro-functions (what one can do). What one can say is in turn determined in terms of the kinds of meaning it is necessary to express. Hence the designation 'notional' in Wilkins' work.[1] This term reflects Halliday's socio-semantic approach, although the use of the word 'function' refers to one of several kinds of meaning, rather than to the level of behavior options as in Halliday. Halliday's views may be represented hierarchically as follows:

Behavior potential (what one can do)
↓
Meaning potential (what one can mean)
↓
Lexico-grammatical potential (what one can say)

The choice of options at each of Halliday's levels will determine what actually occurs in verbal expression. So it is that in the development of syllabus theory it is now proposed that one start with an assessment of what the learner needs to be able to do (the needs analysis), before determining what he will need to mean. Only later does one move on to a consideration of the lexico-grammatical options required. This procedure places a new requirement before the applied linguist: to describe what can be incorporated into a language program to account for the second level, the level of meaning potential. The focus switches, therefore, away from grammar to semantic considerations, and to all the many components of meaning. The 'communicative functions' of language that Wilkins and van Ek identify constitute *one* of these components. They form part of Halliday's 'meaning potential', and are related to Hymes' third component in communicative competence, that is, 'appropriateness'. But they are not, and cannot be, the *only* component of a teaching program. It is important to bear in mind that it was never intended that they should; what was intended was that they should be *included* in any consideration of syllabus development and that they should not continue to be overlooked.

As described by Wilkins, the notional syllabus has as its starting point something different from either the grammatical syllabus or the situational one. Here the syllabus designer concerns himself initially with *what* the student communicates through languages—not with *how* he expresses himself or when or where. What the student communicates is meaning, and so the fully notional syllabus derives from an initial analysis of all types of meaning that can be expressed through language.

Note that there is no intention to exclude linguistic competence, in the sense of knowledge of grammatical structures and the ability to manipulate them, since without such competence there can be no communication. There is no question of sacrificing such competence for communicative competence at all. In the preparation of a syllabus based on the work of Wilkins and van Ek, awareness of *all* categories of meaning must be present. It is this basic reorientation in syllabus design theory, realized in *Threshold Level, Un niveau seuil, Waystage,* and other works of the Council of Europe group of experts, which has such important implications for the teaching of second languages in vocational and professional settings, and which is now also being applied in general education.[2]

The Notional Syllabus: Principles

The idea of the 'notional' syllabus has attracted a great deal of attention; it is also often referred to as 'functional', and in fact the latter term has become more widely known. Various writers use these two terms in different ways, and there is really no agreed usage (see Shaw, 1975, pp.142–3; 1977). The development of this approach to syllabus design however can be traced to the Council of Europe project. In 1971, a group of linguists, now known as the Expert Group, was invited by the Committee of Out-of-School Education of the Council of Cultural Cooperation to enquire into whether it was feasible to create better and more effective conditions for language learning by adults. As the initial reports of the Group were received favorably, their mandate was generalized in 1978 to cover all levels and types of language learning, including schools and universities. They have developed a large and cohesive body of work, the first major volume of which, *Systems Development in Adult Language Learning,* was published in 1973, and contained contributions by Trim, Richterich, Wilkins and van Ek. This volume sets out the principles on which the work of the Expert Group is based, and in accordance with which it has continued to develop its theory.

The first principle is that provision for language learning must be considered as a process of language learning systems development.

Methods and materials for study and teaching cannot properly be considered in isolation, nor can the construction of curricula and syllabuses, or the conduct of tests and examinations. The specification of objectives, the creation of learning materials, the design and conduct of courses following a certain methodology, the accompanying monitoring tests and evaluation have to be seen and developed as interrelated aspects of a single process. Similarly, all course components form a systematic whole. More generally, all stages of education are to be seen as contained within a framework of permanent education. (Trim, 1980, p.108–9).

The second guiding principle is that language-learning systems must be learner-centered. This principle has a number of far-reaching implications. In the first place the choice of language to be learned should be made by the learner as far as possible—Trim does not develop the implications of this principle in the work cited, except to say that as far as adults are concerned there is little resistance to this kind of thinking. He admits that it may be difficult to avoid political or administrative pressures to choose a language in terms of interests other than those of the individual, but he provides no discussion of this particular problem. The interests of children are of course even more difficult to cope with, since it is difficult to accept that they should choose for themselves, yet equally difficult to decide who should choose for them and on what grounds. These matters are of very great interest, of course, but as they are not part of the discussion of syllabus design (which presupposes that the choice of target language has been made) they are not discussed further in what follows.

The major consequence of learner-centered thinking is that planning ceases to be based on language as a self-contained system, and must be carried out instead with the learner's needs, motivations, characteristics, abilities, limitations and resources as the point of departure. Selection from the components of the syllabus will thus be made in terms of the learner, in terms of relevance to his communicative purposes.

Grammatical categories, rules and structures are taught, not simply 'because they are there', like Mount Everest, but in so far as they enable the learner to construct those utterances he needs to achieve his personal and social purposes. (Trim, 1980, p.109).

Note that this does not mean that the course planner and the teacher can ignore the language system. If anything, it means that they must have a very wide knowledge of it, and the ability to be very flexible in applying that knowledge. The teacher's role in particular suffers a dramatic change, and he becomes an agent in the learning process rather than its director—although in this regard Trim cautions that learner autonomy should be viewed as an objective, not as a point of departure.

All this means that the whole system must be needs-oriented. The needs of both society and the individual must be studied, and in particular the specification of language-learning objectives must not be made simply in terms of the knowledge of a certain amount of grammar and vocabulary and a certain level of skill in listening, speaking, reading and writing. Instead, the first question must be what it is that the learner wants to achieve through language. "Language is for use; it is not simply an abstract system for constructing propositions" (Trim, 1978a, p.3). Trim's words are like an echo of the functional views of language that have been current in Europe for many components of meaning that the syllabus designer will have to take into account if he is to proceed within this framework.

Components of the Notional Syllabus

If language is for use, the main unit or component of the syllabus needs to be something other than the linguistic or grammatical one. The two most fully-developed and widely-read arguments against the grammatical unit as the basis for syllabus construction are provided by Wilkins (1976) and van Ek (1975).[3] Wilkins proposed instead the use of 'notion' as the main unit; this idea has been developed principally by him in a short, clear and very influential work. In it he explains that the notional syllabus contrasts with the grammatical and situational types, since it takes the desired 'communicative capacity' as the starting point (p.18). Language teaching is organized thus in terms of the content rather than the form of the target language.

Wilkins explains that the term 'notional' is borrowed from linguistics where it is used in describing grammars based on semantic rather than formal criteria.[4] In the notional approach, three categories are presented, all concerned with general aspects of meaning and use. The three categories thus represent three types of meaning that can be conveyed through language, and are labelled *semantico-grammatical,* *modal* and *communicative function.* The first of these covers the kind of meaning called 'ideational' or 'cognitive' or 'propositional'.[5] It is expressed through grammatical systems in different languages, is also called *conceptional* meaning, and it is fundamental. Both similarity and differences exist among languages, however, and there is thus a close relation between semantics and grammar. The second type, modal meaning, or modality, expresses the *attitude* of the speaker toward his perceptions, his experience. Many linguistic devices are used to express this kind of meaning: grammatical, lexical and phonological. The third category is called communicative function, and refers to the role of the sentence in relation to other utterances that have been produced. This is the part of the interactive process and indicates not *what* is being reported, but what the speaker is *doing* with the utterance.

Of the three categories, the one which is least familiar to the language course planner is of course the third, and the most original and important part of Wilkins' discussion concerns the category of communicative function. But it has been somewhat arbitrarily isolated from the others in attempts to apply notional theory. It is well to remember that Wilkins (1976, pp.23–4) stated that:

> Three different types of meaning have been distinguished and we have designated as a *notional syllabus* any strategy of language teaching that derives the content of learning from an initial analysis of the learner's need to express such meanings. We will find it convenient to refer to the categories of communicative function as expressing *functions* or *functional meaning* . . . whereas the semantico-grammatical categories express *concepts* or *conceptional meaning* . . . it is correspondingly possible to think in terms of a *functional syllabus* and a *conceptual syllabus,* although only a syllabus that covered both functional (and modal) and conceptual categories would be a fully notional syllabus.

Much of the subsequent debate over the implementation of this theory has had to do with whether it is desirable or even possible to separate the categories of meaning one from another for purposes of constructing a teaching program. Furthermore, if it is possible to separate or abstract any one, which should form the basis of a syllabus—conceptual or functional meaning? Or should linguistic form remain as the organizing principle? Many attempts have been made to deal with this problem, of which the present work is one. It remains a central problem in choosing a syllabus type for any given teaching program, and we shall return to it later on. To prepare the way, it will be useful to look at some other models that have been proposed to deal with the question of meaning and the design of syllabuses.

Components in the Threshold Level

Wilkins' colleague in the Council of Europe project, Jan van Ek, has specified a somewhat different set of syllabus components in preparing the 'keystone document' of the Group's work, *Threshold Level*. The 'threshold level' was chosen as the first objective to be defined within the European system because it constitutes "an essential rather than a marginal objective. The large majority of learners who would enter the unit/credit system as beginners would have to pass through this level, whatever their ultimate objective would be" (van Ek, 1975, p.7). They would either be temporary visitors to a foreign country (especially tourists), or would have contacts with foreigners in their own country. They would need a basic level of language suitable for superficial, non-professional contact. *Threshold Level* is an inventory divided into several parts: *situation, language activities, language functions* and *concepts* as well as the linguistic forms required to express the last two of these, and some behavioral specifications.

Van Ek's *situations* comprise "the complex of extra-linguistic conditions which determine the nature of a language act". These include subcomponents of *settings,* social and psychological *roles* as well as *topics.* Language activities for van Ek are what might be called the combinations and proportions of the four language skills required. Language functions resemble Wilkins' communicative functions, but van Ek has included modality in this category instead of treating it as a separate kind of meaning. The fourth component of *Threshold Level* is the behavioral specifications needed, and combines topics and functions. The fifth component is that of general and specific notions. Van Ek's general notions resemble Wilkins' semantico-grammatical category; that is they are notions of properties, qualities and relations. Specific notions, not treated by Wilkins, are more strictly related to topics. Wilkins preferred to exclude what he called the lexical content of learning which should be closely related to subject matter and situation. These were not treated since they are presumably selected in terms of the needs of a particular group of learners and cannot be generalized, whereas van Ek, working on specifications for a particular target group, was constrained to somehow treat them, and did so under the rubric of specific notions and topics.

Van Ek's specifications include, in the last instance, the language forms needed to realize the Threshold Level for English. Up to this point, his definition of content is entirely *non-language-specific,* and thus applicable to any of the languages used within the general socio-cultural context of the Council of Europe. Modifications would have to be made to include certain specific notions and topics (he gives the examples of Spanish 'torero', French 'croissant' and Austrian 'Jause'), but he views these as superficial when compared to the *all-important components of language functions and general notions.* At this point, we see Wilkins and van Ek as basically in accord in giving a central position to these two components.

Van Ek's category of situation echoes Hymes' description of the constituent factors of the speech event (Hymes, 1970), which in turn harks back to Jakobson's theories. While Jakobson moved from the basic triad of addresser, addressee and message, long present in linguistic studies, to develop a theory of language functions, Hymes developed his views in a more sociological direction to include in his list the additional factors of 'channel', 'setting', 'topic' and 'code' and to study their interrelations. In Hymes' elaboration of the speech event the language functions he describes separately are very similar to Jakobson's model, and so include as functions the poetic and meta-linguistic categories which Wilkins and van Ek omit, or at least do not treat as distinct categories.

Linguists and Philosophers

The term 'language functions' then is susceptible of varying definitions. Generally speaking, it has been used in different ways in general linguistics and applied linguistics, where the emphasis is more frequently on the communicative, interpersonal dimensions of language rather than on the more purely expressive or personal ones. In addition, philosophers like Austin and Searle were developing their theory of 'speech acts' at the same time as linguists and applied linguists were devising frameworks to account for what they refer to as language functions. That the philosophers' speech acts overlap the applied linguists' communicative functions has been thoroughly discussed, and their relationships are continually being examined (e.g. Candlin, 1973, p.59). Some applied linguists now prefer to use the philosophical term: for example, Fraser writes that "The first and most obvious answer to our initial question concerning what we do when we use language is the following: we perform speech acts" (Fraser, 1978). This is a somewhat different formulation of language use, and includes the three categories of locutionary acts (the act of saying something with propositional or conceptual meaning), illocutionary acts (the act we perform in saying something, and connected with our intent) and perlocutionary acts (the effect which arises in a hearer as a result of an illocutionary act). The illocutionary act, an act of *doing* something in saying something is that which is of most interest in applied linguistics; the categories Austin suggested most resemble the categories of communicative function proposed by van Ek and Wilkins.

At the present time, the discussion of an appropriate taxonomy continues, as well as how to incorporate these ideas into teaching programs.[6] Differences of opinion in establishing appropriate categories derive from more basic differences in how categories of *meaning* are established, and how many 'layers' there are thought to be. We have seen for example that Halliday proposed three kinds, ideational, interpersonal and textual, which are closely related to his 'functions' or purposes. In the area of functional language-program design, one is concerned principally with kinds of semantic units around which to organize a syllabus. We should now turn to these, and examine further the place of language functions within them.

Speech Events and Speech Acts

In order to determine what van Ek calls language needs, or what Hymes refers to as the constituent parts of language use, one starts by thinking in terms of the situation (van Ek) or the speech event (Hymes). In a situation of speech event, one performs speech acts or one selects language functions, which are realized through linguistic forms, as well as performing other acts of communication of lesser concern to the linguist, but of interest to the ethnologist. Thus, the speech act or language function occupies a mediating position between situation and utterance. Its choice is prompted by the situation and realized through language. The study of the speech act played a central role in applied linguistics in the early seventies, since that discipline was engaged above all in investigating the *communicative* aspects of language learning and language performance. The objectives of teaching had changed, and the learner was to be enabled to select and alter his language with both his purposes and his audience in mind. Candlin (1973, p.107) expressed his view of the matter as follows:

> Such a process will involve actors holding particular beliefs and striking certain attitudes within a variety of roles. In that they will be talking to mean, their verbal purposes are central, modified by the above constraints and that of the settings in which they are realized linguistically. In terms of language description we accept as a result that the meaning of 'knowing a language' has been extended; utterances are to be seen as social acts which exercise effects on the actions and utterances of interlocutors. In terms of language teaching the requirement for syllabuses and materials is that they should lead the learner to be able to transmit information factually and emotionally and to be able to use language instrumentally to get things done.

So far then, the process appears to be as follows:

Speech event or situation

↓

Speech acts or language functions

↓

Linguistic forms.

No matter what taxonomy is used, how many items it includes, or how they are arranged, an account of language functions has to be included in a description of language, and communicative competence has to include the ability to handle a large number of these functions. Whether or not they are all universal, or whether 'macro-functions' are and 'micro-functions' may not be (rather in the manner of van Ek's general and specific notions) is not known at the present time, though these questions are being investigated. Whether they can be arranged in hierarchies of various kinds, for pedagogical purposes, is also under investigation. But no matter what the deficiencies in existing descriptions, language functions are inherent in language description and therefore must be accommodated in a general theory of syllabus design.

Despite the enormous enrichment that sociolinguistic theories have brought to language teaching, and the richness of texture one might have expected from teaching syllabuses drawn from documents like *Threshold Level* and *Notional Syllabuses,* there have been numerous criticisms of underlying propositions as well as disillusionment in translating them into practice. Some result from sheer misunderstanding or lack of acquaintance with the theory; for example, early reactions of hostility seemed based on a mistaken notion that *the* 'notional' or 'functional' syllabus was in reality a new method, whose authors wished it to replace the audio-visual or audio-lingual ones already in place. That this is not at all the case (although the theory has considerable implications for methodology) has become apparent, which may be one reason why syllabus design theory has not had the attention it deserves.

If it is perceived as non-threatening, it is easier to ignore it and go on as before, than it is to embark on the extensive modifications that would ensue from a conversion to communicative language teaching. The argument that we have no account of communicative functions which has been empirically shown to be universal and exhaustive and that until we do, we should not experiment, is also rather weak. Language functions are an inherent part of language; just as language forms were taught for centuries with whatever instruments were available in the form of pedagogical grammars, and the descriptions on which these grammars are based gradually altered, so our teaching should include work on functions.

Realization of a Functional–Notional Syllabus

There was one rather more important consideration of a theoretical kind to be dealt with before it became possible to contemplate the successful implementation of communicative syllabuses. This was that no indication was given as to how to proceed from a list of language functions or speech acts to the construction of a pedagogical syllabus. The same criticism was directed at van Ek's first work on the Threshold Level (1975): while topics and functions were combined in arriving at the behavioral objectives given in that work, no manner of interrelating the other categories was provided (Hill, 1977). The second version of Threshold Level (van Ek, 1976) overcame some of these difficulties, but Wilkins' and van Ek's works generally produced the criticism that the categories of functions and their exponents they had provided were no more than a collection of lists from which only situationally appropriate phrases would be generated, and that what this would yield would turn out to be no more interesting than the phrase books for tourists and businessmen that had been available since the Renaissance.

This was certainly not the intention of the authors in question, and the criticism just cited reflects the fact that while the Council of Europe project has been very well documented, it has not been widely understood. Candlin (1976) made a more useful contribution to the discussion when he wrote that "an item-bank of speech-arts . . . cannot serve any more than sentences as the direct end point of a communicative syllabus", but went on to suggest that we expect learners to do three things: to produce grammatically well-formed sentences and to be aware of intra-sentential semantic identity; to recognize and produce pragmatically equivalent utterances; *and* to 'manage' the interaction. Instruction in grammar will provide for the first ability; the second has to do with awareness of the communicative functions of language and of varieties of language, register, style and the like. The new categories which had been proposed for the notional syllabus, added to those already used in a grammatical syllabus, would provide for these two abilities, as long as a way could be found to interrelate them in the pedagogical syllabus. However, the third kind of ability had not been taken into account, and without it the course designer could not go beyond the stage of phrase book language.

A very severe criticism of notional syllabuses has been made by Widdowson (1979a, p.248) along the same lines as Candlin's.

> The notional syllabus, it is claimed, develops the ability to do this [i.e., realize linguistic competence as communicative behavior] by accounting for communicative competence within the actual design of the syllabus itself. This is a delusion because the notional syllabus presents language as an inventory of units, of items for accumulation and storage. They are notional rather than structural isolates, but they are isolates all the same. What such a syllabus does not do—or has not been done to date (an important proviso)—is to represent language as discourse, and since it does not it cannot possibly in its present form account for communicative competence—because communicative competence is not a compilation of items in memory, but a set of strategies or creative procedures for realizing the value of linguistic elements in contexts of use, an ability to *make* sense as a participant in discourse, whether spoken or written, by the skillful deployment of shared knowledge of code resources and rules of language use. The notional syllabus leaves the learner to develop these creative strategies on his own; it deals with the *components* of discourse, not with discourse itself.

Un Niveau Seuil (Coste *et al.,* 1976) had included one more category than had either Wilkins or van Ek in their visions of the components of the notional syllabus. In presenting the *actes de parole,* the authors of the French version had divided these into five categories:

(i)   *intentions énonciatives,* or those which involve the intentions of a speaker underlying an utterance;

(ii)   *actes d'ordre* (1): utterances which are not a response to other utterances, i.e. initiating utterances;

(iii) *actes d'ordre* (2): responses to initiating utterances;

(iv)   *actes sociaux:* van Ek's 'socializing' function; and

(v)   *opérations discursives:* functions which relate to the discourse itself.

Thus *Un Niveau Seuil* is more than a 'translation' of *Threshold Level;* it adds a vital element to the notional syllabus, one without which it would have been difficult to develop the functional approach very much further. It is interesting to note that the importance of this element of textual cohesion and coherence did not go unremarked in Ogden and Richards, who, in the context of written language, spoke of ". . . the importance of considering the sentence in the paragraph, the paragraph in the chapter, and the chapter in the volume, if our interpretations are not to be misleading, and our analysis arbitrary" (Ogden and Richards, 1946, p.226).

A Further Component: Discourse Structure

The element of the organization of discourse is thus included as an essential component of the functional or communicative approach, and it must also be part of any definition of communicative competence. It represents another layer of meaning, corresponding to Halliday's third 'function'. It will be recalled that Wilkins' taxonomy of categories of meaning has three parts: conceptual meaning, modal meaning and communicative function. Several others have argued that there are four: I have already named Candlin and Widdowson as having insisted on the inclusion of ability to handle discourse, and we should add a reference to the work of Leech and Svartvik (1975) as being extremely important in coming to grips with the need to add meaning in connected discourse, or the textual/discourse aspect of communication as a fourth layer.[7]

If the addition of the ability to create text and in Widdowson's terms, to 'negotiate meaning', with one's interlocutors is added to our conception of the process of verbal interaction, it becomes necessary to add another step to the model of the communicative process given above (p.75).

Speech event or situation

↓

Speech acts or language functions

↓

Discourse skills

↓

Linguistic forms.

A further breakdown of the process is possible (cf. Munby, 1978, pp.45–7):

The speech event or situation

↓

Subsumes communicative activities

↓

In which language functions

↓

Are realized in discourse

↓

As linguistic forms.

The distinction between activities, which together with events belong at the behavioral level, and language functions, which represent the semantic level, helps to explain the confusing grouping encountered in some textbooks, where 'talking about the weather' or 'dealing with an embarrassing situation' (which are activities or topics) are used as unit headings together with 'persuading' or 'denying' (which are communicative functions). The former units must be broken down or processed into functions (Munby's *micro*-functions) before they can be verbalized; the latter are ready for decisions about how they are to be realized in an utterance.

This elaborated conception takes into account social, semantic and linguistic elements; and it also shows their interrelationships in the communicative process. It includes all the elements that contribute to the ability to mean something through language, and reflects the importance of the sociolinguistic work of both Halliday and Hymes.

Additional Criticisms

Two further criticisms of the general approach need to be examined here, before turning to the process of a syllabus design itself. One is that since we have no account of the rules of use (as we have accounts of sentence grammar), we have as a result no basis on which to establish the type of communicative language learning syllabuses that are being advocated. Candlin (1976, p.253) replies to this argument as follows:

> My linguistic reaction is to wonder whether the question is linguistically proper in that it implies a categorialness in sentence grammars that is being undermined, and that I am to infer from it that the equivalent account will do both for syntax and pragmatics. I think that they are different things and that the accounts we give differ as our focus on what we see as language differs.

He goes on to say that as far as pedagogy goes, the learners are themselves analysts of language and will devise their own rules of behavior from approximations to authentic language data that are presented to them in class as well as from their own experience. This is an observation which fits very well with one of the principles on which communicative language teaching rests, that of learner-centeredness and consequently learner-autonomy. And it is a matter to which we will return in the discussion on methodology.

The other criticism comes from Canale and Swain (1980, p.19). They characterize Halliday's claim that semantic options are the realization of social behavior options as 'reductionist' in two ways:

> First, it is obvious that semantic options are constrained by certain aspects of human cognition. Halliday would certainly admit this point but has maintained (e.g. in Halliday 1978) that his orientation and goals in linguistics are socially, not psychologically oriented. Second, we see no compelling reason to give primacy to social behavior options over semantic options in characterizing what one can mean in a language.

Canale and Swain themselves provide the answer to the first criticism: it certainly seems that both psycholinguistic and sociolinguistic approaches to the criteria for language program design are now gradually converging. The second problem (that meaning options may determine social options and that language can be used with little or no reference to social context e.g., self-expression, in poetic language) need not concern the present discussion to any great extent. As Canale and Swain note, Halliday himself made the point that "the more self-sufficient the language (the more it creates its own setting . . .) the less we should be able to say about it in these broadly sociological, or social, terms" (Halliday, 1973).

In the framework of second-language pedagogy, and especially in ESL, we are for the most part concerned with the communicative function of language and not very much with the purely expressive or poetic. That this is not so much the case in mother tongue instruction is clear (see Britton, 1970 and Freedman *et al.,* forthcoming), but most second-language learners are highly concerned with language as social behavior, and that is why Halliday's and Hymes' work provides so many valuable insights in applied linguistic theory.

Converging Viewpoints

In functional or communicative language teaching we agree with Canale and Swain that both the psychological and sociological components of communicative competence must be taken into account in developing appropriate content for a syllabus and in putting it into practice through an appropriate methodology. Psycholinguistic theory suggests that language acquisition is more organic than learned (Corder, 1978b) and that more effective second-language learning will take place if the emphasis is on getting one's meaning across or understanding one's interlocutors rather than on formal accuracy. Sociolinguistic theory suggests that second-language teaching programs should be organized from a starting point of language needs and the kinds of meanings we can express through language rather than that of *a priori* analysis of the target language.

There is no doubt that there are still many unanswered questions in both fields and unexplored connections between the two, such as van Ek's communicative notion of threshold contrasted with Cummins' psycholinguistic view of it (see Cummins, 1979, and Canale and Swain, 1980, p.10). But it would appear that there are strong indications from both sides that the movement to the communicative approach to syllabus design is a movement in the right direction, and one which will provide both better conditions for learning and at the same time a better fit between the purposes (needs, wants, wishes) of the learner and the objectives of the teaching program.

The practical implementation of the theories discussed above forms the subject of the second part of this work which should be understood in the light of these theories. Without a thorough comprehension of the basis of the movement to communicative language teaching, preparation of language teaching programs derived from this approach is likely both to be inadequate and to appear more difficult than it in fact is. If the basic propositions are borne in mind, however, practising teachers should be able to prepare a communicative syllabus which will prove invaluable as a planning instrument.

Notes

1. Munby (1978) provides a helpful discussion in which he explains that as an applied linguist he is working within a theoretical perspective that will be derived from a theory of communicative competence, rather than from one particular linguistic theory. I think he is quite right in this assessment of what the difference between a theoretical and an applied framework needs to be. See especially his diagram (1978, p.20) which indicates some of the complexity of the field for those interested in 'competence'.

2. It must be noted, however, that what we have been given by Wilkins and the Council of Europe team in these publications are mainly tools for the construction of a notional syllabus (and two or three proto-syllabuses to suite particular circumstances). Any pedagogical syllabus which is based on these works must select and order from the inventories provided in them and available elsewhere. It is not possible to create classroom-ready materials without going through the procedure of further selection and sequencing, a procedure which will be discussed in chapter 5 of the present work.

3. The idea of 'notions' and of 'communicative potential' are present earlier than 1975 in the various documents published by the Council of Europe Expert Group. See Shaw (1977, p.226–8) for a brief survey and bibliography of the Council of Europe papers to 1975, and Appendix I of this work for a list of the most prominent and accessible publications now available.

4. See Simon Dik, *Functional Grammar* (1978), for a description of the formal and functional paradigms.

5. Wilkins immediately points out the use that Halliday makes of 'ideational', and asserts that Halliday's three-fold division of 'functions' does *not* parallel Wilkins' model of the division of meaning into three types.

6. An examination and comparison of the taxonomies of communicative functions and of speech acts present in the literature in applied linguistics would represent a major undertaking now. A quick look at Wilkins' and van Ek's taxonomies is enough to indicate that their general categories are different yet interwoven. To illustrate: one of the listings under van Ek 'Expressing and finding out intellectual attitudes' is "expressing how certain/uncertain one is of something", which shows up in Wilkins' category of modal meaning under 'personalized scale of certainty'.

7. See Munby (1978, Chapters 2, 8) for a comparison of levels of meaning in the work of Wilkins, Candlin and Leech and Svartvik.

Part Two:
SYLLABUS DESIGN IN THEORY AND PRACTICE

Chapter 5:

Language Program Development

THE PROBLEMS which face those who are responsible for language course design are complex. More complex than they used to be.

The reasons for this state of affairs lie in the changes in theory which I have discussed in Part One of this book. The inclusion of the criterion of appropriateness in planning language courses has caused an upheaval in the traditional approach. The disturbance was already being felt a good 10 years ago when Pit Corder, for example, made it clear that the profession was facing a number of problems (Corder, 1972). He stated that the relevance of both descriptive and comparative research in linguistics to the specification of the *content* of a language course was well enough understood, and that the methodology of these procedures was also well established. However, Corder went on to say that the next stage in the application of linguistics to language teaching, or what he called the tertiary application of linguistics, was at that time less well researched and understood. This is the stage at which the content of the language course, once specified, is organized or structured into a syllabus.

The chief difficulty in syllabus construction in the last decade has been to discover whether it is possible to include consideration of socially appropriate and communicative use of language as well as linguistic structure and general usage. If this issue can be resolved, the further question of how to implement a communicative syllabus still has to be examined. It is complex; yet when ways can be found to handle the many strands which constitute such a syllabus, teachers have at their disposal a very much richer curriculum to work with. All the approaches which have so far appeared may be ranged on a continuum. At one end, very detailed and fairly rigid specification of content may be the rule. At the other, no specification of content at all is advocated.

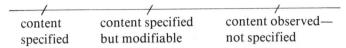

| content specified | content specified but modifiable | content observed—not specified |

There is a middle position, becoming quite widely accepted, according to which syllabus content is indeed set out in advance of the beginning of a course, but in which varying degrees of flexibility are maintained.

As well as situating the many models of syllabus design which have appeared in recent years at points along this continuum, one may also describe them as more or less communicative, depending on whether they include more or less emphasis on the communicative functions of language. There are various other factors to be taken into account in describing syllabus types, but before looking at them more closely it might be as well to examine the overall process of language program development. When it is clear where the choice of a syllabus type fits into this process, it will be time to examine in greater detail some of the models which have been reported on so far.

The Components of a Communicative Syllabus

The principles on which a syllabus is structured are different from those for selecting the linguistic content to be included in it. The former involve consideration of a number of extra-linguistic factors, having to do with the educational setting in which the course is to be taught, the characteristics of the learners, the circumstances in which the educational institution operates, even the society in which the language-learning and teaching process is to be carried on. This means that if we now wish to make up the deficit in earlier syllabus types, and ensure that our learners acquire the ability to communicate in a more appropriate and efficient way, we have to inject a larger number of components into the make-up of the syllabus. These components could be listed as follows:

1. as detailed a consideration as possible of the *purposes* for which the learners wish to acquire the target language;
2. some idea of the *setting* in which they will want to use the target language (physical aspects need to be considered, as well as social setting);

3. the socially defined *role* the learners will assume in the target language, as well as the roles of their interlocutors;

4. the *communicative events* in which the learners will participate: everyday situations, vocational or professional situations, academic situations, and so on;

5. the *language functions* involved in these events, or what the learner will need to be able to do with or through the language;

6. the *notions* involved, or what the learner will need to be able to talk about;

7. the skills involved in the 'knitting together' of discourse: *discourse and rhetorical skills*;

8. the *variety* or varieties of the target language that will be needed, and the levels in the spoken and written language which the learners will need to reach;

9. the *grammatical content* that will be needed;

10. the *lexical content* that will be needed.

Notice that of the ten components listed, two only (9 and 10) have traditionally been considered essential. The others have been included sporadically and unsystematically, if at all, since they were either not considered as part of the planning task in second-language teaching or at best peripheral to it. Within current theories of how the language teaching operation should proceed, a consideration of most, if not all, of the ten components listed is viewed as being necessary (van Ek, 1973; Wilkins, 1976; Munby 1978; Trim, 1978b). A number of syllabus types, labelled according to which of the many components listed above receives most prominence, have now emerged. Among those that have been most frequently discussed are the structural or grammatical syllabus, the situational syllabus, and the functional–notional syllabus. Each of these is constructed according to different principles, and each needs to be understood by the syllabus designer. The kind of syllabus that incorporates a consideration of all ten components is increasingly referred to as 'communicative', since it takes into consideration everything required to assure communication. The matter of which component receives most emphasis is negotiable within the constraints of any given teaching situation.

Stages in Program Development: The Needs Survey

In order to understand the process of constructing this type of syllabus, it is best to start at the next higher level in the language-learning/language-teaching process, that is by examining the overall process of planning a second-language program. Within this framework, the syllabus is seen as only one part of the whole, although a very important one. A diagram of the stages in language program development is shown in Fig. 5 and Table 5. A detailed analysis of the steps it represents in planning and implementing a syllabus will occupy much of what follows. First, however, we need to develop a more general appreciation. On examining the outline, one sees readily that the specification of syllabus content (or what I prefer to call with Alexander (1975) a 'proto-syllabus') is produced in Stages III and IV. Having a syllabus is therefore not the same thing as having teaching materials and lesson plans at the ready. It should also be clear from the outset that the diagram has been drawn up in terms of stages and that these are represented as discrete operations for the sake of clarity. In the discussion which follows, it will become plain that there must be a constant flow of information from one stage to another, and that in fact the stages often overlap.

As can be seen from the diagram, the first stage in the process is two-pronged: it entails carrying out a survey of the communicative needs of the learners for whom the program is being prepared as well as a survey of the physical resources at hand. The concept of a needs survey comes to us from the work of the team of experts which the Council of Europe assembled in 1971 to study certain linguistic problems confronting the European nations at the time of the creation of the Common Market. There were shifts in population as groups of workers travelled north to work in countries whose languages they did not

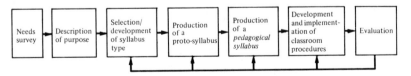

Fig. 5. Language Program Development.

TABLE 5. *Stages in Language Program Development*

Stage	Description
I	Needs Survey
II	Description of purpose to be prepared in terms of 1. student characteristics 2. student skills on entry to and on exit from the program
III	Selection or development of syllabus type in terms of IV and physical constraints on the program.
IV	The proto-syllabus: description of language and language use to be covered in the program.
V	The pedagogical syllabus: development of teaching, learning and testing approaches. 1. development of teaching materials (as far as possible) 2. development of testing sequence and decisions on testing instruments
VI	a) Development of classroom procedures 1. selection of exercise types and teaching techniques 2. preparation of lesson plans 3. preparation of weekly schedules b) Teacher training: briefings or workshops on 1. principles 2. desired outcome 3. exploitation/creation of teaching material
VII	Evaluation 1. of students 2. of program 3. of teaching
VIII	Recycling stage 1. congruence or 'fit' between goals set and student performance is determined 2. content is reassessed 3. materials and methodological procedures are revised

necessarily speak. At the same time, much greater mobility between countries was being planned for individuals in various occupations and professions. The possibility of establishing a 'unit/credit' system of teaching modern languages to adults was being studied,[1] and the communicative needs of the workplace were seen as being paramount.

As it was initially conceived, the needs survey was closely tied to the language needs the worker would experience in another country during the exercise of his occupation or profession; thus, specifications made for course content were based on detailed studies of these kinds of language needs. In recent years, linguists have greatly refined this procedure, and have conducted surveys in industrial and professional settings in order to determine very precisely just what learners for whom a given course was being prepared would have to do through the language once they were actually on the job. Needs specifications have been made for a good many vocational and professional settings, and abundant reference may be found to them in the literature under rubrics such as 'vocational English', 'industrial English', 'English in the work-place' or 'in the market place'. There are even more particular designations, such as Candlin's well-known studies of doctor–patient interaction (Candlin, Bruton and Leather, 1976), which have formed the basis for course materials for doctors needing to learn English. It has been said (Germain, 1979) that this sort of survey produces a very narrowly focussed set of specifications—as indeed it can and should if the goal is to prepare the learner as quickly as possible to get and keep a job.

The needs survey does not have to produce such a limited set of specifications, however. Everyone has communication needs and wishes; but they are not always necessarily related to a particular occupational setting. There is no reason why this kind of survey cannot be carried out for each and every group of learners, whether or not the course is to be designated GELP (General English Language Program), or ESP (English for Special Purposes), or EST (English for Science and Technology), or VESL (Vocational English as a Second Language), or by any of the numerous abbreviations one meets in the literature.

Indeed, the whole *concept* of needs analysis has been considerably extended and enriched, after a good deal of experimentation, criticism and re-evaluation. It now includes the identification of the communication requirements, personal needs, motivations, relevant characteristics and resources of the learner. It also includes investigating those of his 'partners for learning' (Trim, 1981): teachers, employers, administrators, family and friends and colleagues, and even those of materials writers and textbook publishers. The line between needs and wishes is now quite indistinct, and may be unnecessary. For purposes of the present work, however, a distinction may be made between 'needs' as externally imposed and reflecting one's ability to operate as a member of society, and 'wishes' as being internally generated, having to do more with personal aspirations.

The Needs Survey in General Education

In carrying out needs analyses, the most clearly described and most accessible work has been done for courses responding to occupational requirements (e.g. for Jupp and Hodlin's *Industrial English,* 1975). But needs analysis can be considered equally well in two other broad areas: in general education and in preparing the general interest or 'survival' course. Taking the first of these, it has been argued that for courses in general English, for example in secondary schools in non-English-speaking countries, it is unnecessary to depart from the standard syllabus which consists of a list of grammatical structures and a list of vocabulary items to be taught. It is often felt that if the learners gain command of the grammar of the language, communication will come in good time. It is also argued that it is too difficult, even impossible, to determine what the learners' communicative needs will be. As a result, one might as well equip them with the full range of grammatical resources and let the rest come later.

After much discussion of these issues, an attempt was in fact made to discover whether the communicative needs of school-children could be assessed. That they had specific needs which could be defined in such a way as to be useful in the design of a syllabus has been uncovered in at least one well-known instance, and the results published as *The Threshold Level for Modern Language Learning in Schools* (van Ek, 1976).[2] As one might expect, the communicative needs of school-children using a second language as the medium of play and instruction are related very directly to two areas of activity: topics and language functions appropriate to interaction on the playground and in the classroom. Furthermore, the children's needs relate closely to other subjects in the curriculum, and it is therefore possible for example to think of a course in English as a second language at the school level which would incorporate topics drawn from history, geography, social studies and so on, as well as from general culture and literature.

As an extension of this view of communicative needs, one might well conceive of a series of courses in a second language given in a college or university setting (to assist students to gain the kind of skills they need to be able to perform successfully in those settings), in which topics would be drawn from the appropriate academic disciplines. That this is in fact possible is recognized by the existence of a body of literature devoted to the design and preparation of courses in EAP: English for Academic Purposes. A second and powerful reason for considering revision of syllabuses in general education is that the addition of components from the larger lists of possibilities mentioned above constitutes a considerable enrichment of the range of themes, topics and activities in teaching, and thus makes for more interesting classes—a desirable end in itself.

The Needs Survey for 'Survival' Courses

The second broad area in which the needs survey can be applied is that of the 'general interest' or 'survival' course, the kind given to individuals who need a basic command of the language for immediate, everyday requirements. But why should one conduct a survey of the particular needs of a group of students in a general-interest program? Surely in a situation where one is teaching this kind of 'survival' English, or 'English for social purposes', the needs are sufficiently generalized to make this step unnecessary? Often this is not the case. The teacher may make decisions *on behalf of* the learners concerning what interests are general enough for them all, or in which situations the learners will have to survive. But even in this kind of program, a needs survey can yield some interesting, often unexpected, results. It does not have to be as detailed a survey as for an EST course, for instance, but well-placed questions will often make the difference between a course expressly designed for one's students and something so general as not to interest anyone.

A recent report on conversation class activities illustrates the fact that teacher expectations about topics that will provoke lively discussion are often dashed by student reactions of utter boredom (Urbanic, 1979). It should also be borne in mind (a point to which we will return in Chapter 6) that conducting a needs survey is not to be conceived of as having the learners fill out a questionnaire. Indeed, if they are beginners in the language, they would be incapable of doing so. It involves obtaining information by asking questions about them and on their behalf—something the designer of the syllabus ought to be able to do as part of the process of getting to the final stage of class-room interaction.

Within these two broad categories of course design (general education and general interest), there is always the possibility of more refined specifications. The syllabus may be as broad or as narrow as one can or will make it. Thus, one hears of English for secondary school children in parts of Canada where Cree is the first language, or of English for tourist guides in Cairo, or of English for mothers of pre-school children, recently arrived in the United States from Indo-China. These courses will evidently vary enormously in content and in focus. But they can all start from an examination of the communicative needs and wishes of the learners, and they should all be based on a syllabus, rather than proceeding on an *ad hoc* basis from day-to-day or even hour-to-hour.

Further Stages

From the needs survey, one progresses to the preparation of a description of purpose, and information gathered during the first stage of program development is incorporated into it. In some cases, the description of purpose is entirely dictated by the needs assessment. This would be the case in courses for specific industrial or vocational purposes, for example. There is however a more difficult operation to perform when the needs are not solely professional (Germain, 1979). In certain situations the syllabus designer might be constrained to add other elements (such as study of the culture associated with the target language) which might not come out of the needs survey quite as directly as, for instance, the need to know how to answer the telephone. Nonetheless, this task can be carried out quite effectively in the vast majority of situations. Furthermore, if one is using a syllabus rather than a 'method', the process of continual evaluation is quite possible, and one can refine at will the description of purpose of the course, and thus the syllabus itself. We will return later on to this aspect of program development.

Once the purpose of the language-teaching situation under consideration is determined, one should proceed next to determine the type of syllabus that would be best suited to the needs and characteristics of the learners. While a full discussion of syllabus types follows in Chapter 6, a few preliminary remarks may be in order here. It certainly seems that a Proportional Syllabus—one in which there is a balance between emphasis on form and emphasis on communicative functions— is desirable in the majority of cases. There are nonetheless some situations which may call for a fully structural syllabus, and we should most certainly not exclude this possibility from consideration. This is why the diagram of Language Program Development (Fig. 5) contains a box corresponding to this stage, since the description of purpose (which derives from the needs analysis) will not automatically yield a description of syllabus type. It is up to the program planner to decide what will be best at this point.

Fortunately the concept of syllabus design is much more flexible, far less rigid, than it has been. This is not surprising, since what is now occurring is that the procedures of communicative syllabus design, originally designed for application to situations in which needs and purposes could be quite narrowly specified, are being applied to the preparation of more general courses. The model of syllabus design thus becomes a dynamic, not a static one, and it allows for constant feedback from a variety of points into the area of syllabus type and selection of content, as well as into other areas such as teaching procedures.

To return to the procedure under discussion. When the general syllabus type has been decided upon, one moves on to produce the proto-syllabus with the aid of a number of instruments in the form of lists or inventories. The next stage is to develop overall approaches to teaching and learning (including teacher training) and also to the whole testing program. Finally, the syllabus designer shares his responsibility with the classroom teacher, who is, as always, responsible for conducting, supervising, and encouraging classroom interaction.

The Syllabus Designer and the Teacher

It is worthwhile at this point to digress briefly, to clear up the confusion that sometimes arises when one tries to delineate exactly what the roles of the syllabus designer and classroom teacher ought to be.

The syllabus designer works squarely in applied linguistics. Now, new definitions of applied linguistics are vastly more complicated than the one which was used when the term first began to come into current usage in the '50s and '60s. The number of components or sources of input into the discipline has increased and the relationships among them are very complex. A corollary of the several theories of what applied linguistics is or should be is that the role of the applied linguist (and his training) is different today from what it was a number of years ago. Formerly, the linguist himself 'applied' his theoretical knowledge to the creation of pedagogical grammars, in the belief that better pedagogical grammars would be the key to better language training. Therefore, when his primary task was to create better teaching grammars, the theoretical linguist was, or could be, an applied linguist. The applied linguist today, however, has a more complicated task, and must draw on more sources of information to help him succeed. The applied linguist who works in second-language learning and teaching is concerned principally with what is to be taught, how it is to be taught, and inevitably with the process of language acquisition. The applied linguist, in other words, is critically concerned with the designing of syllabuses for teaching programs (Corder, 1973).

The role of the classroom teacher in models of the type we are discussing also requires some clarification. The applied linguist is concerned not only with what is to be taught and how it is to be ordered (the syllabus), but also with the realization of the syllabus in the form of teaching materials such as textbooks, exercises, tapes, filmstrips and so on—that is, with the *presentation* of the syllabus, or what might be called the development of the pedagogical syllabus (Stage V). While the language teacher is also concerned with teaching materials, he is so in a different way—his concern should be with exploiting them in the classroom. He deals with teaching techniques, artistry in the classroom (Stage VI).

Language teachers may of course also function in the role of applied linguist (insofar as they draw on the principles of linguistic science in their activities), and some applied linguists are in fact also language teachers. One person may be either or both, but it is important to note that the *roles* are differentiated. This notion may trouble some teachers, who do not feel they are able to wear the applied linguist's hat. Yet what is stated above would probably be acceptable if one were to suggest that the classroom teacher often has—and wants—responsibility for planning the curriculum. The point is that in planning the curriculum—or more accurately, designing the syllabus—for a second-language course, one ought to be drawing on linguistic principles. To the extent that one does (however limited), one is acting as an applied linguist.

Evaluation and Recycling

Returning now to the process of developing a language program, it can be seen that the final phase is evaluation, which has two broad aspects. First, one would wish to evaluate or test the students in the program; next, the teaching as well as the over-all design of the course should be assessed. The applied linguist and the classroom teacher must work especially closely at this stage. Finally, there is the recycling stage in which the fit between goals set and the final performance of the learners is determined. If there are discrepancies, as there often are, materials and teaching approaches are revised, and in some cases the description of purpose is re-examined with a view to establishing whether or not it should be altered in light of the results obtained at the end of the program. This is labelled the 'recycling stage' because the whole cycle can be begun again at this point, and adjustments made anywhere in the system based on the feedback provided to the syllabus designer. As long as this stage is retained, the model is flexible and dynamic. Without it, the procedure is rigid and unresponsive to any sort of change or reassessment.

The whole sequence outlined above may seem rather forbidding to anyone attempting it for the first time. Indeed, one may feel one is being encouraged to abandon everything one has been doing so far and start again from scratch. In fact, this is not the case; nothing of the sort is necessarily implied in the adoption of a communicative syllabus. The designer himself controls how much or how little command of any of the language skills being included will be required, and how they will be taught. What is being advocated is the enrichment of our current language-teaching programs by including consideration of speech acts or language functions, and by gearing the content as closely as we can to the language needs of specific groups of learners. We can shift the emphasis as we wish, from structural to communicative aspects of language and back again. For example, we can come up with a syllabus of 'variable focus' (Allen, 1979), in which we begin with the emphasis placed squarely on structural considerations, as it has been in the past, and then gradually arrange for the focus to change to communicative needs, and eventually phase into teaching *through* the language.

Changing an Existing Program

In any case, one does not always start from scratch. In many situations in which the introduction of a communicative approach to second-language teaching is being contemplated, it is more a question of having to modify an existing program than building up a whole operation from the beginning. Rather than ignoring what is already in place, and attempting to prepare a new syllabus without any reference to it, another approach is desirable. An examination of the syllabus currently being followed can be undertaken, and used as the basis for an altered syllabus which can have a different focus. Sometimes the outlines of a syllabus may appear only through the tables of contents in textbooks being assigned in a course of study; even in such cases, the linguistic content at least will have been partially determined.

Discussions with teachers and further examination of teacher-produced materials will also reveal that in fact certain notions, topics, situations and language functions are already being covered, though not always systematically or thoroughly. The final syllabus may then be prepared by comparing the material covered in a current syllabus with the needs of the learners as determined through a needs survey. (We must assume, of course, that a needs survey would be undertaken regardless of whether the decision was to produce a new syllabus or to revise an existing one.) It is then a relatively manageable task to fill in the gaps in the syllabus itself, and to go on to produce and select teaching materials to cover the areas which were omitted previously. It should also be noted that the adoption of a particular syllabus type does not *necessarily* imply a change in methodology. It has implications for the presentation of the content of the syllabus (in other words, for the *product*), but the selection of types of exercises and drills, whether or not to use audio-visual aids, the role of memorization, do not constitute the point of departure in the design of a syllabus. Materials must be harmonious with the syllabus type selected, but one does not start the process with the materials; rather, one proceeds by selecting from the components mentioned above, then by ordering the items selected. The choice of materials comes later.

The procedure used to generate a revised syllabus is the one shown in Fig. 6 and Table 6. The process which it exemplifies can be carried on while existing courses continue to be taught. Furthermore, there is

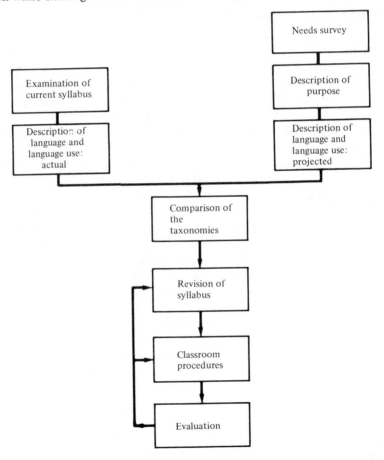

Fig. 6. Language Program Modification.

no reason why teachers may not begin to introduce parts of the new syllabus into their classrooms in the form of modules or units before the entire revision of the syllabus is complete. In fact, once the process of adaptation is begun, it is quite likely to continue for some time, since the syllabus designer will presumably be interested in having some feedback from the classroom (bearing in mind always that the syllabus designer and the teacher could very well be one and the same person, though the roles are differentiated). To recapitulate, the whole process is seen as reflecting a dynamic and flexible relationship among all the stages of program development.

TABLE 6. *Stages in Language Program Modification*

Stage	Description
I	Description of purpose in terms of 1. student characteristics 2. student needs 3. language skills on entry and on exit

II	Design of a Communicative Syllabus
	Phase One: examination of the existing syllabus
	1. extraction of current taxonomies of
	  a. linguistic form
	  b. lexis
	  c. language functions and skills
	  d. notions and topics
	  e. situations
	  f. other components
	2. Sequencing of items thus identified
	3. Comparison of current taxonomies with proposed taxonomies
	Phase Two: the revised syllabus
	4. Preparation of revised taxonomies for the whole curriculum.
	(From this point onward, the stages required to complete the process are the same as those in Language Program Development, Table 5.)

Notes

1. In September 1971 the Council of Europe set up a group of experts which agreed to concern itself with the following tasks:

    (a) to breakdown the global concept of language into units and sub-units based on an analysis of particular groups of adult learners, in terms of the communication situations in which they are characteristically involved. This analysis should lead to a precise articulation of the notion of 'common core' with specialist extensions at different proficiency levels;

    (b) to set up on the basis of this analysis an operational specification for learning objectives;

    (c) to formulate, in consultation with the Steering Group on Educational Technology of the Council of Europe, a meta-system defining the structure of a multimedia learning system to achieve these objectives in terms of the unit/credit concepts (Trim *et al.*, 1973, p.9). Credits were to be given for units; a European language diploma would be the goal.

2. The Ministry of Education of the province of Quebec has also undertaken a needs analysis in English as a second language for the fourth and fifth years of their secondary level (Gouvernement du Québec, 1980). As the syllabus which derives from it is still being turned into classroom interaction it is difficult to say as yet how successful the needs analysis will have been.

Chapter 6:

Designing a Communicative Syllabus: Stages I-III

Now THAT a general model for language program development has been set out, we need to develop further the procedures involved in stages I–III, all of which precede classroom work. They comprise the needs survey, the description of purpose, the selection of a syllabus type, the preparation of a proto-syllabus and finally its realization as a pedagogical syllabus, ready for the classroom teacher to begin work on.

Stage I: The Needs Survey

Once the decision is taken to proceed along communicative lines in the preparation of a language-teaching program, a needs survey, followed by the production of a description of purpose for the program, are necessary initial steps. When a needs survey is being undertaken there is potentially a great deal of information to be gathered. The extended definition on p.90 includes communication requirements, personal needs and motivations and relevant characteristics of learners, as well as those of their 'partners for learning'. The reason for all of this information gathering is to understand as much about the learners as possible prior to the beginning of the program, in order to establish realistic and acceptable objectives. Past tendencies in language program design have been to start at the beginning of the whole language system, in the hope that the learner would continue until he mastered it all. In other words, a primary objective was to lay a good foundation.

With a more contemporary approach it may be said that in many cases it is preferable to start at the end, with the specification of program objectives and work back, bearing in mind always that one is producing a *limited* description of the target language. We are now more prepared to accept this notion than ever before, even though a good deal of information which is not yet available would be useful in the process. Guntermann (1980) points out that questions such as what the appropriate roles and behaviors are for foreign-language learners, and what the target levels in socio-cultural as well as linguistic proficiency should be, are as yet unanswered. Until more information is in our hands, defining target levels of communicative ability for academic as well as occupational courses will be a tentative operation. In the meantime, since a return to a strictly linguistic or structural approach is unlikely, we shall continue to press ahead in developing better instruments for the analysis of needs.

In a discussion of this issue, Holec (1980a, p.26) reminds the reader of how needs analysis has been seen:

> Needs analysis is by now the classical procedure by which a close link can be established between learners and curricula: whereas in content-centered approaches, learning objectives are defined in terms of quantitative subsets of the total communicative competence of a native language user, in learner-centered second language instructional systems, the selection of objectives is based on the particular communicative needs of groups of, or individual, learners. Such a procedure makes it possible to set up curricula perfectly adapted to particular learners, especially if the assessment of needs is not just carried out once and for all before the beginning of a course, but is repeated regularly over the learning period.

"However", he continues, "the success of this procedure depends on just how the learner's needs are analyzed". The difficulties attendant on arriving at a finely-tuned needs analysis are numerous (see, for example, Mareschal, 1977; Bibeau, 1979; Germain, 1980; Guntermann, 1980), and various systems for dealing with the collection of data have appeared. Of these, Richterich and Chancerel (1977) and Munby (1978) are the most highly elaborated. The procedure is now well enough established, given the current state of knowledge in this area, and the chief danger has been identified as that of isolating needs analysis from the other components in language program design. If it can be part of the flexible approach described above, separation of needs analysis from concern for the learner's aptitude, learning strategies and personal interests need never take place, and the needs analysis—or survey—can continue to make an appropriate contribution to syllabus and materials design.[1] Thus it is that Richterich, who fathered the classical conception of needs analysis, now states that we would be better to speak in terms of an *assessment of available resources,* including those that the learner brings with him to the classroom experience (Richterich, 1979, 1980). In this way, the concept is vastly extended beyond its initial definition.

A major difficulty in implementing a communicative syllabus has surfaced in discussions of more general language courses, in which it has often been said that school-age learners have no needs at all. As I pointed out above (chapter 5, p.92), there is some evidence to the contrary. It is better to think in terms of discovering, together with one's students, areas which suggest at least *potential* communicative requirements. These could include both classroom needs (classroom language) and those which may come in future vocational or recreational pursuits. The needs survey can also include the learner's own desires or wants, seen more subjectively in terms of self-expression and less in terms of purposeful or transactional communicative behavior.

It is preferable, then, to start off by thinking about the reasons for conducting a needs analysis rather than about cut-and-dried procedures. The object is to obtain as much information as possible in any given situation about the learners and about their purposes in acquiring the target language. *What* one wishes or is able to find out may vary; and exactly *how* one goes about this is also likely to vary quite considerably from one occasion to another. One may obviously wish to consult the learners themselves, but this may not always be possible, either because of a language barrier (in the case of beginners), or because they simply are not there to be consulted (in cases where planning must be undertaken prior to their arrival on the scene). In such instances, one would try other avenues: friends and relatives or sponsoring agencies; indeed, any contacts at all might be exploited.

Data Collection

In preparing to carry out a needs survey, it is helpful to know something of the approaches to data collection to which I have referred. A checklist is often used to guide an initial needs survey. Note that it should normally cover two broad categories: who the learners are (what they bring with them) and what their purposes, needs and wishes are in learning the language (where they are going). Note also that checklists are planning instruments designed for use by the syllabus designer. They are not questionnaires. They are bridges between a potentially enormous and exhaustive list of information that one might be able to amass, and an infinite number of worksheets or questionnaires that might be developed for use in specific situations. Some examples of questionnaires, worksheets and grids are provided in Mackay and Mountford (1978), Clark (1979), Kross (1979), Harlow *et al.* (1980), Dos Gahli and Tremblay (1980), Mackay and Palmer (1981), Pierson and Friederichs (1981). Many of these were developed from lists and inventories of forms. One which was designed to be given directly to students and filled out by them (with help from their instructors) is included in the appendices to this book (Personal Data Sheet for EAP), together with a checklist of the sort which is frequently used as a guide in needs surveys.

Working from a checklist, the syllabus designer can produce a variety of procedures to be used in the needs survey, or survey of resources. In addition to those just mentioned, he may wish—he *should* wish—to include face-to-face interviews, as often as possible and with a variety of individuals. In this context, not only the learner's needs may be surveyed, but also those of the individuals with whom the learner will be interacting: future colleagues, superiors, contacts of all sorts in the socio-cultural environment in which he will be using the language (the 'partners for learning'). It is of course impossible to predict each and every contact that might be made, but it is not impossible to produce an educated guess.

Just how precise one's description of the learner's characteristics and of their role-sets (i.e. the set of individuals with whom they will interact by virtue of their role in the target environment) will be depends on the resources the syllabus designer has at his disposal with which to carry out the job: time, contacts, funds, etc. And the format in which the needs survey will be reported will also vary. An example is to be found in Appendix IV, and the literature provides a number of models ranging from those which follow Munby's procedure very closely (e.g. Carroll, 1980, p.106) to some which are reported in a more narrative style (e.g. Yalden, 1980a). Regardless of actual format, the needs survey will serve as the springboard to the next step in the process, and will evidently influence subsequent decisions and directions.

Stage II: The Description of Purpose

With the needs survey complete—or at least well under way—the next step is to clarify the purpose of the language program. This will establish the foundation for the major decision facing the language course designer when he arrives at Stage III, the selection of a syllabus type. Initially, of course, this did not appear to present a problem.

In the early literature on syllabus design—which admittedly was not large—one could detect a tendency to refer to '*the* notional–functional syllabus' as though there were one and only one model. Until the mid-'70s, this was thought to be the case: the differences between Wilkins' *Notional Syllabuses* and van Ek's *Threshold Level* were often overlooked. Now, however, there is no single theory of communicative syllabus design, but many. Differences lie in varying conceptions first, of what the objectives of a language-teaching program should be, and how they should be stated, and second, of the methodology that should be employed. But these differences cannot be described as neatly as were the contrasts among methods, since a syllabus can be anything from a real blue-print for turning out teaching units or materials to a set of rather broad guidelines.

After a considerable amount of debate, there seems to be general agreement that the blue-print definition, typified by Munby's Communication Needs Processor (1978), is appropriate only for language courses which have highly defined purposes, and that the less structured approach will serve better in the case of courses with a wider scope. In other words, the more accurately one can predict what the learners' language or communicative needs will be, the more clearly the content of a syllabus can be delineated. In more general courses, too close a specification can lead to suffocation of initiative and interest.

In this light an interesting distinction is made by Robinson (1980) between English for *Special* and English for *Specific Purposes,* suggesting that the former is thought to refer to restricted languages (for example, that of air traffic controllers), which for many people is only a small part of 'ESP', whereas the latter focuses attention on the purpose of the learner and refers to the whole range of language resources. This corresponds to the distinction we make here between courses which have a narrow focus, prepared for a highly homogeneous group of learners who will have very clearly defined language needs in an occupational setting, and courses which might be classified as being for educational purposes. In the latter category, courses may either be for study in a specific discipline or may be given as a school subject. In neither case would language itself (whether seen as the self-contained system of structuralist theory or as the route to cognitive and cultural development of the grammar-translation tradition) be the sole subject matter, nor would its mastery be the sole objective of the course.

While an appropriate degree of mastery is obviously a necessity, it will be based on a limited description of language. Appreciation of the system *qua* system is not always considered necessary. The idea of *specific purposes* implies only that there is a limit to the amount of time the learner can spend on the task, and that it is accordingly necessary to select certain aspects of the target language which will be given special prominence in the preparation of the syllabus. It does not imply that the learner will be forced into a straitjacket of set phrases, and sent forth with only a sort of special code to be used in highly structured situations. It is important to bear in mind as well that in more general language courses the content of what Clark calls an 'input' syllabus can only be scientifically determined to a very limited extent. It will be necessary instead to proceed rather more intuitively, since the variables of actual performance when the target situations are not precisely defined or definable cannot be catered for on a one-to-one basis between needs and language (Clark, 1979, p.103).

Occupational and Educational Purposes

We can thus agree with Strevens (1977, 1980) when he proposes two large functional groupings in teaching language for specific purposes (Fig. 7): *occupational* or *educational*. (Mackay and Mountford, 1978, propose three—occupational, vocational and academic—but Strevens seems to do the job as well with a more restricted terminology.) These are important distinctions to be borne in mind during Stage II in language program development, since they will have a bearing on further stages, and will help to focus the process of producing a well-defined description of the purpose of the program.

Mackay and Mountford (1978), Robinson (1980), and Strevens (1977–1980), all provide excellent discussions of these distinctions, and Mackay and Mountford also present useful case histories. Until very

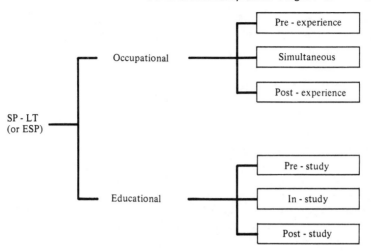

Fig. 7. (From Strevens, 1978).

recently, however, not much detailed discussion of syllabus theory has been provided, no doubt because either the Wilkins–van Ek model or the Munby model was being applied and not very much time had been given to development of alternative models, (see, however, Bachman and Strick, 1981, and Johnson, 1982). In the last few years, several other models have been suggested, all of which are less rigid than either van Ek or Munby, and reflect the concerns that Wilkins had expressed about the applicability of the fully notional syllabus.

Generally speaking, these later models are conceived of as being broad guidelines which *can only be realized in a given situation.* Each situation may contain different objectives (that is, a different balance of skills, modes, content and so on) as well as different teaching activities (formal, functional, experiential) to develop communicative competence of a particular kind. Thus, Moirand (1981) refers to *minimalist* and *maximalist* implementations of the communicative approach, according to how large a view is taken of communicative competence. In preparing the description of purpose to be produced for a given course, the language program designer will accordingly work in terms of broadly or narrowly focussed purposes, and occupational or educational categories. These distinctions are present also in the design of the syllabus and in the choice of exercises and activities for its implementation.

Stage III: The Choice of a Syllabus Type

After deciding on the general category for a course, the next step in the design of the syllabus is the choice of a syllabus type. There is, as we have already suggested, no single model of syllabus design which is universally agreed upon. Thus the question of the interrelationship of the components of a syllabus is a difficult one. Solutions that have been proposed range from a modification of existing structural syllabuses to a completely learner-centered approach in which there would be no 'prospective' or 'input' syllabus at all, but only one which would grow out of the situation as the course progressed. Methodological implications permeate these discussions: they also range widely from a focus on structural and functional analytical exercises, to functional and structural 'activities', to strictly communicative activities based on authentic materials rather than specially written ESL texts. Various combinations are possible, and of course various focuses on oral or written language, as required, are also feasible.

In examining syllabus types, we begin with Wilkins' original definition of the dichotomy between an 'analytic' and a 'synthetic' approach to syllabus design (Wilkins, 1976). The analytic approach can generate a number of possible syllabus types. Two broad categories have been discussed above (Chapter 4): the situational and the functional. The latter can be seen as including a number of subcategories, all distinct from the situational syllabus-type in design, and there has been considerable confusion in the terms used to describe them.[2]

Wilkins (1978) has explained the matter in the following way: it is possible to follow various paths in the design of an analytic syllabus constructed to teach language use. Wilkins called the *strongest* approach to syllabus design 'notional', for in it *all three categories of meaning* (ideational, modal and communicative) were woven together. All are expressed through a knowledge of the grammatical, lexical and phonological systems, and of how to make appropriate choices from items available in each.[3]

It should be recalled that in his initial discussions of analytic syllabus types, Wilkins commented that global or general courses were not the best field of application for the notional approach, since general courses were regarded more as an investment for the future. In specialized courses, he felt the notional syllabus to be highly appropriate, since a course designed to incorporate all three kinds of meaning would have a 'high surrender value'.[4] That is to say, that whatever was learned could be used at once, in contrast to the delay customary in a general course, where the learner had to wait until he had absorbed a considerable amount of structure (usage) before he could attempt to use the language for effective communication. This distinction is of course the one referred to in the discussion of Stage II, the description of purpose. It comes down to the difference between a ESL course for an occupational or for an educational purpose.

It might appear that the language teacher is no better off now than he was during the debates on methods. If anything, the configuration of variables that have to be taken into account in preparing to teach a second-language course may seem more confusing than ever. However, lest the reader abandon all hope at this point, we should point out that a great deal of very successful work has been done in designing syllabuses which take into account form, topic and function, and that this has been done (in part at least) by refusing to be entirely bound by any of the three basic syllabus types so far discussed (structural, situational or functional).

Many of those who have been working with these ideas have come to the conclusion that what is now required is a more flexible approach to syllabus construction. One should feel freer to emphasize those elements or components which any given teaching situation demands. The best way to refer now to describing a classroom experience which more closely approximates an environment of real language use is through use of the term *communicative*. Syllabuses designed for such situations should thus be called communicative syllabuses. Assuming that a decision has been made to orient a language-teaching program in a more communicative or semantic direction, away from a purely structural or grammatical base, a choice among options has to be made. There are several possibilities, depending on the learner's objectives (or those set on his behalf). Any of those described below might be chosen: they are all considered to be forms of the communicative syllabus.

Communicative Syllabus Type 1: Structural–Functional

At first glance, the weak functional or structural–functional syllabus, as defined by Wilkins, is the easiest solution to the problem of communicative syllabus design. It has wide application: a separation of the two components of form and communicative function is maintained, and it is thus relatively easily implemented. The point at which the teaching of communicative function is included might vary somewhat; it would, however, always be assumed in working with this model that linguistic form had been treated quite thoroughly before work on language functions was introduced. It is thus a question of adding a further component to an already existing syllabus, rather than integrating communicative teaching with teaching linguistic form. It could be a useful model to use in reorienting an existing structural course. Those designing general courses will wish to be aware that Wilkins, writing in 1974, was of the view that notional and functional considerations might for the time being be regarded as simply providing another dimension to existing grammatical and situational syllabus components. The new dimension, he felt, could prove especially valuable in a general course *where the aim was remedial,* i.e., beyond the beginners' level.

> A notional approach can provide a way of developing communicatively what is already known, while, at the same time, enabling the teacher to fill the gaps in the learner's knowledge of the language. In either case the learner will have an awareness that he is doing something fresh (Wilkins, 1974, p.121).

Communicative Syllabus Type 2: Structures and Functions

The second communicative syllabus type represents a *structural progression in a communicative framework.* Brumfit, who has criticized the notional syllabus in all its manifestations, proposes a different solution. He argues that Wilkins has not addressed the question of learning theory, and that it is therefore difficult to see on what grounds he proposes the reorientation of second-language teaching.

> Whatever criteria we use [in syllabus design] . . . principles of organization must be answerable to a view of how language is learnt. It is on the basis of a view of

language learning that systematizability and motivation are seen as important criteria for the selection and ordering of items (Brumfit, 1981, p.91).

Brumfit argues that since cultural and linguistic meaning is customarily negotiated between users of a language, it is more sensible to provide them directly with the tools for this negotiation (the linguistic system) rather than teaching them what to do with the tools. His solution then is to retain form (grammar and pronunciation) as the organizing principle since we can successfully generalize about it, but not about what people should do and mean. Paulston (1981) also supports this view, as does Valdman (1978, 1980). However, none of these writers would wish to imply a "contradiction between emphasis on analysis and discussion of facts about language and languages, on the one hand, and imparting of a certain level of communicative ability, on the other" (Valdman, 1980, p.83). They all have been mainly concerned with syllabus design for global courses, serving general educational objectives. Valdman goes so far as to argue that these courses cannot aim solely or even primarily at the imparting of communicative competence.

Brumfit describes his model as follows (Fig. 8):

> The simplest proposal is to use the grammatical system as the core of the syllabus in a ladder-like series of stages and to be prepared to relate all other essential material to this series. Thus notional, functional, and situational specifications can be conceived of as a spiral round a basically grammatical core (Brumfit, 1980b, p.5).

Syllabuses have to be concerned with both accuracy and fluency. Yet at the early stages the conditions for achieving one are incompatible, in Brumfit's view, with conditions for achieving the other. He advocates development of communicative *methodology* to help develop fluency as well as accuracy, while maintaining structural progression as to the organizing *principle* of his syllabus type. This model then is not the same as Type 1 since all components of meaning are to be included from the start—none are to be postponed.

Brumfit's treatment is complete and consistent; and he is not alone. Johnson's (1977a, b) argument for what he terms a communicative rather than a primarily functional syllabus fits into the same category. He believes (a) that functional organization implies structural disorganization; (b) that assigning functions to utterances is difficult, as

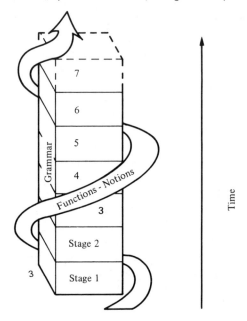

Fig. 8. (From Brumfit, 1981)

more than one may occur in any given utterance, thus making the production of functional *units* of teaching materials difficult; and (c) that a choice of exponents[5] is daunting, given the large numbers which are possible for each function (Halliday provides sixteen ways to scold a child; Wilkins gives two pages of exponents for asking permission; deByser, 1980, draws up a lengthy inventory for expressing disagreement; and so on). Johnson (1977a) suggested as a result that the best way to proceed in general courses was for the gradual and small development of functional material to be integrated with existing language teaching programs. He also proposed an interesting approach to this gradual development, in line with Brumfit's appeal for more communicative methodology.

> Under such a scheme coverage of the common core might be provided by a series of teaching units each containing theme-specific and language practice materials . . . alongside materials with a functional orientation. Each unit would

cover a separate theme area, and the theme-specific source text would serve as the point of departure for both language practice and functional materials. To this extent the theme area mode of presentation now used would be retained.

There seems no reason why a specific sequence for the presentation of the three material types within each unit need be fixed, though the fact that the source texts are to provide the stimulus for language practice and functional materials will clearly impose some restrictions on the ordering. Nor should the material types necessarily appear as separate parts of the unit: it would be possible (for example) to move from theme-specific materials to what has been called 'language practice', return to theme-specific followed by functional materials, ending up with more language practice (Johnson, 1977a, p.677).

The *unit of organization* is thus central to Johnson's model, and considerations of methodology of vital importance. He discusses a variety of types of unit, each providing a different focus for what could be the same content (Johnson, 1982, pp.55–69). Thus, units can be given functional, notional or structural focus, and all used in conjunction with a structural core if desired. Adopting this approach, one might also be able to move increasingly toward a functional emphasis, while retaining a structural progression, and at the same time producing a richly varied series of units.

Communicative Syllabus Type 3: Variable Focus

Johnson's work leads to a further conception of syllabus design, in which shifting emphasis takes place according to level in a progression from elementary to advanced, rather than in a given unit. Structural progression as well as structural exercises and activities would dominate at the first level, and the emphasis would then change to communicative function and finally to situation or subject-matter. Peter Shaw (1979) suggested a model of this kind at the level of over-all design, rather than in the context of levels within a single course. Yalden (1980a) presents the description of an EAP program constructed in a similar way, in which the progression is from a common core component, to an English for Academic Purposes component with a strong functional emphasis, and then to monitored participation in specially arranged courses given in English which simulate the true academic situation. The most complete discussion, and the one which provides the name for this model, is to be found in Allen (1980), where the author describes a three-level 'variable focus' ESL syllabus for secondary schools in Ontario. Emphasis shifts in turn (from structural work on formal features of language, to rhetorical (discourse) features, to the instrumental use of language in the study of school subjects. Allen (1980) explains the concept as follows (Fig. 9):

> Although the structural foundation model has a useful role to play in ESL curriculum, we believe that it should be interpreted in a way which allows for the maximum amount of flexibility in materials design. This can be provided by making use of the concept that 'grading should be the focus rather than exclusion' (Allen and Widdowson, 1974a). Thus, at level 1 the main emphasis is on structural practice, and functional and instrumental practice will be, relatively speaking 'out of focus'. Similarly level 2 emphasises functional practice, and level 3 instrumental practice, but at both levels the other types of practice remain in the background ready to be utilised as the need arises. By making use of a variable focus technique we give recognition to the fact that there are three types of practice (structural, functional, instrumental) which interrelate, which are interdependent and which co-exist at all levels of language learning. At the same time, the notion of 'primary focus' ensures that at all times the lesson content remains under control and adaptable to the needs of the student at any given level of proficiency.

Levels of Communicative Competence

Level 1	Level 2	Level 3
Structural	Functional	Instrumental
Focus on language (formal features)	Focus on language (discourse features)	Focus on the use of language
(a) Structural control	(a) Discourse control	(a) Situational or topical control
(b) Materials simplified structurally	(b) Materials simplified functionally	(b) Authentic language
(c) Mainly structural practice	(c) Mainly discourse practice	(c) Free practice

Fig. 9. Three Levels of Communicative Competence in Second-Language Education (Allen, 1980).

Communicative Syllabus Type 4: Functional

For this type of syllabus, objectives are stated primarily in terms of communicative functions, not in terms of linguistic items or in terms of ideational content, although these components often are included and sometimes obscure the purpose of the syllabus design. In this approach, the objectives determine the functions needed, and the functions determine the selection and sequencing of grammatical materials. The work of Jupp and Hodlin (1975) exemplifies this approach, often used in occupational or vocational ESL. It also appears in approaches reported by Mills (1978) and McDonough (undated) in courses for college-level students (EAP). Language practice *derives* from the objectives, leading to Johnson's complaints of structural disorganization. The *unit of organization* is *functional* in this kind of syllabus, and once a pattern is developed such units can be turned out quite readily with a little practice. (They are further discussed in Chapter 8).

Many EST courses and materials have been based on the functional approach; they have been criticized for providing 'phrase-book language', or for teaching only 'language-like behavior' rather than developing communicative competence. However, in situations where rapid progress to a highly functional variety of the target language is essential, this syllabus type can be extremely valuable. The reader will again wish to examine the literature in the area of languages—especially English—for special and/or specific purposes for full discussion and examples. (See especially Robinson, 1980).

Communicative Syllabus Type 5: Fully Notional

The fully notional syllabus, as defined by Wilkins, remains the strongest possible approach to the input syllabus. *Threshold Level, Waystage* and the other Council of Europe documents exemplify it in all its complexity; Munby's (1978) extensions and elaboration of the work of Wilkins and van Ek provided a further model for generating a fully notional syllabus, suitable for learners whose proficiency in the second language has to be specified for very particular and essentially narrow purposes. Maley (1981) presents a contemporary version in which all components (socio-cultural, semantic, linguistic as well as psycho-pedagogical) are braided together (Fig. 10).

These works have been discussed above as the inspiration for subsequent models and do not require elaboration here. Instead, we turn to a brief discussion of the end of the continuum which was referred to at the beginning of the section on Syllabus Types: the learner-centered model.

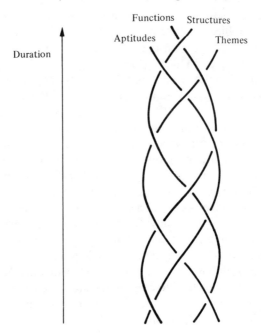

Fig. 10. (From Maley, 1981).

Communicative Syllabus Type 6: Fully Communicative

The *learner-generated* or *fully communicative* view of syllabus design is one in which there would be only the most minimal input syllabus, if indeed even that. It has arisen principally out of a concern with methodological problems and their solutions. Alexander (1975) pointed the way to some of these in an essay entitled "Some Methodological Implications of Waystage and Threshold Level" where he indicated that in using the Council of Europe documents, the syllabus designer had had to develop his own framework for a course, and that the simpler the utterances to be taught, the more complex the framework had to be. He discussed some of these frameworks, or what we call syllabus types, but stressed that all courses based on 'functional–notional' models must take as their starting point that communication must be taught and is therefore the primary objective. (The reader may wish to compare Alexander's taxonomy of frameworks with the one offered here.)

It is not surprising that, faced with the difficult and complex task of syllabus design thus portrayed, and in attempting to implement the communicative approach in general education in which needs and target levels are hard to describe, some applied linguists have advocated a solution in which the extent of teacher involvement in, and direction of, the process of language use in the classroom would be drastically curtailed. Those who subscribe to this approach generally show a strong preoccupation with methodology, teacher preparation and learner autonomy, considering these to be the cornerstones of language teaching, rather than the input syllabus. Newmark has demonstrated these concerns in his work for some time. Thus, he has spoken of "the exponential power available in learning in natural chunks", and even discussed ways of making both acquisition and learning (in Krashen's sense) as independent of live teachers as possible with complete self-instruction in the *use* of language becoming feasible as well. He has also criticized "present psychologically oriented pro-grams" as well as structurally oriented ones for the artificial and apparently inevitable isolation of parts from wholes. He comments that:

> The odd thing is that despite our ignorance as experts, as human beings we have always known how to teach other humans beings to use a language: use it ourselves and let them imitate us . . . we have no compelling reason to believe with either children or adults that the method is not both necessary and sufficient to teach a language (Newmark, 1966: reprinted in Brumfit and Johnson, 1979, p.163).

Allwright (1979, p.167) extends the defence of a minimal language teaching strategy by arguing

> that if communication is THE aim, then it should be THE major element in the [language teaching] process. The question could be put:
> Are we teaching *language* (for communication)?
> *or*
> Are we teaching *communication* (via language)?

Allwright, like Candlin and Breen, does not imply that the two are incompatible, but rather that linguistic competence is a *part* of com-municative competence. If we focus on communicative skills, we will inevitably develop most areas of linguistic competence. If we focus on linguistic skills only, or even primarily, we risk failing to deal with a large part of communicative competence, however that may be defined. To accomplish the former, Allwright advocates having the teacher's 'management activities' directed exclusively at involving the learners in 'solving communication problems'. In so doing, language learning would take care of itself.

This point of view leads away from the notion of a well-developed plan of action in the form of a syllabus, to the point where it is difficult to consider it an approach to syllabus design in the usual sense at all. However, it might be possible to think of negotiated syllabuses at least for adult learners, in which the learner would have a good deal to say both about content and about learning strategies. If this were possible, self-direction would be necessary at all stages, including the definition of objectives and the choice of pedagogical techniques, as much as in the monitoring of learning procedures (Holec, 1980b). This is a radical proposition with far-reaching implications in methodology, and it has been suggested, first, that it is not possible during the early stages of language learning, and second, that learners have to be led towards autonomy as they are not accustomed to it nor do they expect it in language learning situations.

Other Types

There are yet other syllabus types being elaborated which are not described here as they are still in a developmental stage, and in any case are treated elsewhere. (See, for example, Johnson, 1982, for an interesting description of some of these approaches. His discussion includes the 'procedural' syllabus, a type which is entirely task-based and replaces the linguistic syllabus completely.)

Is it possible to reconcile the views presented above by means of a single framework for syllabus design? In the following chapter we examine this question and suggest a tentative solution which practising teachers and those now responsible for syllabus design may find helpful.

Notes

1. Holec (1979, 1980) provides a comprehensive discussion of the relationship between these two aspects of syllabus design.

2. Initially, this group was known as 'notional', but the use of this term gave way to 'functional', due to an excessive emphasis given to the place of communicative functions in some of the literature, and the use of the term 'notional' has not gained as much currency as has 'functional'. For Wilkins, the *weakest* approach to syllabus design was to teach structure first, then functions. This is what he originally meant by 'functional', but this is now only one example of what is today called 'the functional approach'. Others are described below.

3. On the matter of the categories of meaning, there is now disagreement: some writers feel that the notional or ideational strand needs no special identification in the syllabus, since one cannot avoid it. Others feel that *specific* notions are simply 'topics', which have generally been included in syllabuses everywhere and therefore need only to be included in the usual way without further ado, while *general* notions so permeate the lexico-grammatical structures of language that there is no need to identify them separately.

4. 'High Surrender Value' is a term borrowed from the language of insurance policies, and refers to a term policy on which there is a high rate of return.

5. The exponents of a function are any and all of the linguistic items which are used to realize it in a given language.

Chapter 7:

The Proportional Approach

A WIDE range of communicative syllabus types have been devised in the period since the group of experts assembled by the Council of Europe began their work. It seems most unlikely that any one of the models proposed will be universally accepted. The emergence of a universal type of input syllabus is no more likely now than the emergence of a universal method of second-language instruction. One must look elsewhere to provide guidance for language teachers. Furthermore, despite the difficulties associated with the implementation of a communicative syllabus, all the indications are that learners will come increasingly to want communicative language courses.[1]

A communicatively oriented language teaching program need not be dominated by any syllabus types described above. It is of course possible to choose one or another, especially for very short courses. For longer courses, or for sequences or levels of instruction within a structured curriculum, a balanced or *proportional*[2] approach would seem to allow the syllabus designer the most freedom to respond to changing or newly-perceived needs in the learners, and at the same time provide a framework for the teacher who may not be able or willing to 'go fully communicative' and enter the classroom with nothing save a collection of authentic material. A proportional syllabus comprises a large number of possible variations and can be implemented in most of the second-language teaching situations with which we are familiar.

The Principle of Balance

An early version of this approach appeared in Yalden (1980b), and illustrated the balance one might seek in designing a general EAP course. The model then proposed reflected the conviction that once one is committed to the teaching of communicative function in a second-language program, it becomes almost impossible to postpone such teaching for very long. Thus, Fig. 11 illustrates the balance which one might seek in designing a general ESL course at an elementary level of communicative competence. One might wish to begin with grammar and pronunciation (the formal area) only, but introduce work in the language functions (the interpersonal area) and discourse skills (textual area) fairly early and in time increase emphasis on this component. The study of grammar would nonetheless remain in sharper focus throughout the first level than would the study of functions and discourse skills. If the focus shown in Fig. 11 represents that of the first level, in a sequence of courses, the one shown in Fig. 12 could well be adopted for the next level. Here we see that the teaching of the textual area gains increasing prominence as the course progresses, but the teaching of grammar also occupies an important place. In the third level of a hypothetical course sequence of this sort one would expect the balance to have shifted again, and for the proportions to be represented as in Fig. 13. At this point in the sequence, work on the communicative functions of language predominates, and one would expect linguistic form to be considered only as the need arose. This bears some resemblance to the functional–structural model described earlier, the main difference being that it does not constitute a point of departure but rather a stage to be reached in a balanced progression. That progression may take place at varying rates, and within one course. The figures are illustrative of the proportions that may be contemplated; they are not restrictive. Putting the three figures side by side makes the overall plan evident. While both formal and functional areas have their place, linguistic form is gradually de-emphasized and communicative functions and discourse skills are given more prominence as teacher and student progress toward the end of the advanced level.

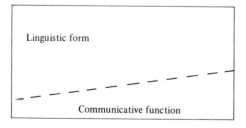

Fig. 11. The Elementary Level in a Balanced System.

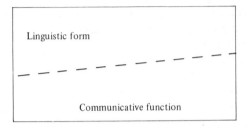

Fig. 12. The Intermediate Level in a Balanced System.

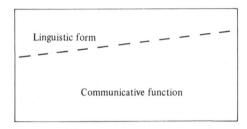

Fig. 13. The Advanced Level in a Balanced System.

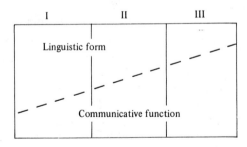

Fig. 14. Three Levels in a Balanced System.

In the representation of the relationship between the emphasis given to kinds of meaning in a syllabus, the whole area of notions and topics (the ideational layer of meaning) is not shown as a separate component. The choice of a given number of topics is inevitable in today's teaching, as very few individuals would advocate a return to teaching grammar and vocabulary items without stressing a situation or context in which they might be used. Topics, general notions, situations, themes can therefore be seen as the framework which provides support for the rest of the components which are included. Topics and situations suitable for a syllabus for adolescents or adults will arise from a needs survey undertaken as part of the process of planning the syllabus; this component is thus the least troublesome of the three to fit into the design of a syllabus.

In using a balanced syllabus, it would have to be borne in mind that there need not be a strict separation between teaching formal and functional areas. The divisions shown in Figs. 11–14 represent differences of proportion in time allotted to the teaching of each component. They do not indicate that the two must be kept separate; indeed, it is assumed that it is for the most part impossible to do so. This principle, together with that which permits shifts of emphasis or focus onto different components of communicative competence, or different pedagogical strategies according to circumstances, leads to the development of the proportional syllabus (Fig. 15). In this conception the selection and implementation of different approaches to syllabus design at different points in the preparation of an overall language-teaching program is permitted.

The Proportional Model

The proportional model includes the provision of an initial phase, principally comprising formal and ideational layers of meaning. This phase is for complete beginners, and need not last long, but it seems essential to provide some basic knowledge of the systematic or categorial side of language before one can expect learners to go on to a more interactive mode of learning. Absolute beginners cannot be expected to solve communication problems (Allwright, 1979, p.170).

Allowance is thus made in this model for the difficulty of broaching communicative functions with learners who have no knowledge at all

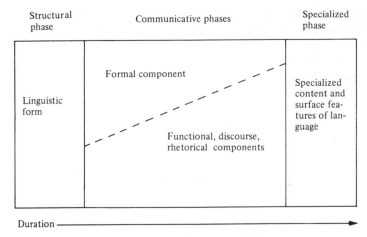

Fig. 15. The Proportional Syllabus.

of the target language. It also accommodates the position that although communicative competence includes linguistic competence, it is possible to teach grammatical competence *before* teaching sociolinguistic competence. The proportional model permits a change, nevertheless, to emphasis on speech acts and discourse skills in oral language at a relatively early stage, by retaining the idea of balance from the model shown in Fig. 14. Once communicative work in oral language has been attended to sufficiently, it is possible to shift the emphasis once more: at more advanced levels, the syllabus designer can include emphasis on rhetorical functions, especially in written language, as well as on recurrently troublesome features of surface language. A return to some work on form (to the synthetic approach, in other words) is allowed for once communicative performance is under way. Finally, the model can be extended to include more purely instrumental or experiential learning in subject areas.

Selection and Sequencing

What of the question of selection and sequencing? We referred in Chapter 5 to the need to select items from lists or inventories as being part of the job of the syllabus designer. Once these items are selected, the further problem of their arrangement in the syllabus specifications awaits. It is well to recall here that while the formal area of language will continue to be taught in any communicative program, it does not have to be done in the customary manner of 'taking the learner progressively through the forms of the target language' (Wilkins, 1976). The question of exactly what kind of progression should be followed is not yet resolved, but there still is support for the notion of approaching the linguistic component of communicative competence systematically rather than unsystematically. For one thing, in dealing with adults, language *learning* ability must be taken into account by all parties to the process, and it is the target linguistic system that is the most obvious problem, the most different from the native system. Furthermore, though language in actual use shows extreme structural diversity, this diversity is not altogether typical of actual language-learning situations.[3] Thus, while a syllabus (or a component in a syllabus) which is focussed on system does not have to follow strictly any of the approaches to the question of progression which have been used to date, it can still be systematized. One needs to work out an approach "which is grammatical because it is communicative and communicative because it is grammatical: an integrated approach which is based on the recognition that acquisition and use are not distinct but complementary and interdependent aspects of the same process" (Widdowson, 1978b, p.11).

It is more economical to arrange for systematic treatment of the formal component, but the treatment will now be spiral or cyclical rather than linear in order to accommodate other components of communicative competence. Corder (1973, p.297) describes this approach to the teaching of second languages as follows:

> In its more sophisticated form it means returning to some more general area of syntax or semantics, for example, or some domain of language use, developing a deeper or more abstract understanding of the items, processes or systems involved, relating them and integrating them with the other material already presented and learned.

There is a good deal of research in verbal behavior which supports the spiral approach (for a brief review, see Martin, 1978). The practice of an item distributed over a period of time leads to better retention than if the item had been practised once and then set aside. Recall is strengthened, furthermore, if an item is encountered in a different context each time (a process known as differential or variable encoding). It is as though the student were given many and varied opportunities to rehearse the items, rather than just one exposure to them. The spiralling of grammar has received attention in recent years (Martin, 1978); the spiralling of semantic, functional and formal components in a language course has also been discussed (Mohan, 1971; Finocchiaro, 1979); but is still not as familiar to most teachers as it might be.

In preparing the grammatical component of an input syllabus, one or more of the traditional bases for ordering a structural syllabus might be used (for example, contrastive analysis for pronunciation if the group of learners is homogenous, and error analysis for aspects of syntax), but the teacher would expect to return to material previously presented and expand on it in successive lessons. Other criteria have also been suggested for sequencing the grammatical system. Canale and Swain provide five categories in addition to the criterion of grammatical complexity: transparency with respect to the communicative function of an utterance; generalizability to other communicative functions; the role of a given form in facilitating acquisition of another form; acceptability in terms of perceptual strategies; and degree of markedness in terms of social and geographical dialects (Canale and Swain, 1980, pp.21–22). Morrow (1977b) also discusses this problem, providing still other criteria.

Nonetheless one of the main difficulties for the second-language learner remains grammatical complexity, which ought to be carefully considered *in relation to the other aspects* of the syllabus. Since these other aspects will in turn be considered in the light of a needs survey, it is not possible to provide any more clear-cut guidance at the present time, and tried and true handbooks of grammar will very likely continue to be used by syllabus designers, teachers and learners as before. If the linguistic system is not approached systematically and the learner's progress goes unmonitored, there exists the potential for fossilization at too early a stage, and progress towards a desirable standard of grammatical accuracy may be forestalled.

The structural core or spine would be present in the communicative phases of the model for syllabus design under discussion here, but not all of the teaching would be by any means focussed upon it alone. On the contrary, one would expect a variety of exercises and activities, of which formal exercises focussed on grammatical structures would represent only one kind. In a 'fully communicative' or procedural syllabus type, no formal or analytic exercises are included; in the proportional syllabus, there will be a *range* of exercise types including formal exercises treating linguistic structures and formal exercises focussing on functional aspects of language (including rhetorical skills); as well as communicative activities focussing on either structural or functional or semantic aspects of language. The notion of changing focus is central to this approach to syllabus design, and the concept of a basic unit which is used as a pattern or template to produce an infinite number of lessons is rejected. In addition, the components of communicative competence are expected to be braided together far more tightly than they are initially as progress is made into the second and third phases of the syllabus.

System and Non-System

The question of how to sequence the elements identified as necessary or useful in the proto-syllabus remains a difficult one. Much has been made of the fact that there is no authoritative list of speech acts, that their combination in speech events has not been sufficiently studied, that we therefore cannot describe discourse systematically, and furthermore, that we do not know which speech acts are universal and which are not. Johnson (1980) has pointed out that there can be two positions taken on this very basic problem: Widdowson's view that certain components of communicative competence are as yet unsystematized which suggests that one proceed cautiously; and Candlin and Breen's claim that these components are not susceptible to systematisation at all. Johnson himself probably provides the best solution to this problem when he suggests that although Candlin and Breen's 'nature of communication' arguments may not convincingly dispose of the notion of a systematic component, they are important for a number of related reasons, one being that they lead one to think in terms of *some combination of system and non-system.*

> One might well conclude that in the same way the insight that there is an unsystematisable element of communicative knowledge sets limits on the feasibility of systematic teaching, so the existence of system in language sets limits on the necessity for process-type teaching (Johnson, 1980, p.9).

The kind of combination required is one in which we will need to redefine our teaching in order to make sure, first of all, that more learned language (in Krashen's terms) finds its way into the acquired system by providing more effective kinds of classroom language (Krashen's 'intake'). Second, acquired language needs to be *used,* consolidated, to use Johnson's term. We thus reject both 'globally non-systematic' *and* 'globally systematic' approaches, accepting, on the contrary, that there is a highly systematic element in communicative competence—the linguistic component—and a number of unsystematic ones as well. Communication is unsystematic and unpredictable, but we use systematically learned and organized language to achieve it. This systematically-learned language needs to become part of the language system used as unconsciously as possible. To achieve this end, communicative activities now being proposed provide us with the "activation techniques" (Johnson) which have so far been missing from our repertoire as teachers.

The combination of these systematic and non-systematic components is thus the domain of the syllabus designer and empirical research could well turn to this question. Some combinations have been represented as broad syllabus types, but there are many other possible arrangements to be studied. Any given syllabus could consist of a number of segments of varying focuses: formal–informal or systematic–non-systematic in nature, and centered on form, function, rhetorical skills, themes and topics, as needed. Johnson (1980) provides a 'sequential' solution to the problem of system vs. non-system whereby the non-systematic areas could be treated in terms of the needs survey, and thus reflect the learner's own wishes and desires and the language needs he would have as a potential member of an occupational or professional group.

1. Non-system → system
2. System → non-system
3. Cycles of non-system → system
4. Cycles of system → non-system

This concept contrasts clearly with 'simultaneous' solutions, of the type offered by Maley. Johnson notes, however, that problems may yet arise, since if there is a strong relationship among various areas of the syllabus in terms of semantic content, the non-systematic component easily becomes a vehicle for practising systematically-learned language—and is perceived by the student as such (Johnson, 1980, p.13).

Varying the Proportions

Given the present state of our knowledge, the proportional approach would seem to constitute the most viable framework for communicative syllabus design. Since it consists of a number of connected segments, the boundaries between formal and communicative teaching approaches may be varied to suit the requirements of the situation. No doubt the debate over the composition of the segments of a proportional syllabus will have to continue for some time before anything more certain can be said about the validity of one kind of sequence as compared with another. Nevertheless, the approach is a highly adaptable one in general or EAP courses. Taken together with the flexibility we have advocated regarding specification of content, it can serve as a powerful generative device for the production of classroom material. The time devoted to the systematic (linguistic) component of communicative competence and the non-systematic ones (meaning, communicative functions, discourse skills) may be similarly varied.

A variety of suggestions have been offered on the sequencing of the non-systematic components. Choices are probably best made according to local requirements rather than waiting for a definitive answer. Some solutions that have been offered are extremely helpful, and provide the syllabus designer with a number of interesting possibilities. One of these non-systematic components may be labelled 'interactive skills' which include the ability to choose appropriate functions and to weave them into a text. Teaching skills of this nature may be approached primarily through the classification of communicative functions, one possible continuum being that of predictability. One might then choose to emphasize those functions which are most predictable. (In speech, ritual functions head the list, with initiating functions next, and response functions at the end. Response functions are the least static, since they build on what one's interlocutor has said.) One might also wish to examine dominance as well, since in any speech act there may well be more than one function present, and it may be necessary to identify those which are most important, or carry the greatest force.

One might then emphasize Wilkins' macro-functions (Wilkins, 1981), and help the learner to develop the ability to shift emphasis from referential to directive, for example.

Guntermann and Phillips (1981) suggest three further criteria for selecting functions: immediacy of need (classroom functions), generalizability (to other situations) and complexity (of form). This is a practical approach which could be very helpful in the process of syllabus design for general courses, and provides a flexible approach to the question of sequencing functions.

In order to prevent the treatment of functions as isolates in the teaching process, it is of course desirable to follow Widdowson's advice that we should relate teaching activities to authentic samples of discourse. There is now a large literature on the analysis of discourse which shows how second-language teaching can be enriched by inclusion of exercises and activities based on real texts, spoken as well as written. The kinds of texts studied will furnish ideas for work on rhetorical functions and discourse skills. These appear to be other non-systematic components, except insofar as work in discourse analysis has revealed the presence of patterns of logical arrangement of ideational content in certain subject areas (see, e.g. the *English in Focus* series for examples of how subject matter and discourse skills can be related).

An interrelated progression in conceptual and linguistic skills for ESL at the secondary level has been outlined by Allen and Howard (1981), moving from a lower and more descriptive level (concerned with When, Where and How), to a higher and more analytic one (concerned with Why):

> The language work associated with explanatory analysis will be more complex than that associated with descriptive analysis. Activities appropriate at the higher level will include such communicative functions as expressing cause–effect relationships or arguing a point of view and providing supporting evidence (Allen and Howard, 1981, p.540).

The same functions (cause–effect, suasion, etc.) have been integrated with some success into modules for use with learners at a 'high beginner' level in college preparatory program in English for Academic Purposes (Young and O'Brien, 1979). The constraints of age make the difference here: acquiring a social competence may be relatively easy for adult learners whose culture is not far removed from that surrounding the target language. (See Fraser, 1978, and Bott, 1980, for interesting discussions of this question.)

Varying the Methodology

It is evident that there are many unexplored areas left in syllabus design, including the question of how prescriptive one ought to be about methodology in preparing the proto- and pedagogical syllabuses. Clearly one can no longer talk in terms of 'the' syllabus or 'the' method. But as long as we think of shifting focus or emphasis in the proportional syllabus, we must also think of shifting or varying methodology. Allen has suggested three 'focuses': structural, functional and experiential. Each of these seems to require different teaching approaches, or methodologies, on the surface of things, but as Johnson suggests we may be able to devise teaching techniques which will treat all three types variably as well.

Are our students to be given different doses of ideational, functional and textual medicine at different times—or can we mix the three together? This question resembles the problem of sequencing components of the language system, and many and varied prescriptions will doubtless be offered as the communicative approach takes hold. The need to keep the elements discrete decreases after the initial purely structural stage is past, and there ought to be a long period during which a richly varied methodology is desirable. This in turn could well be capped by a series of diversified courses in which the elements still needing attention are specially treated, both formally and informally as needed. This represents the final stage of the proportional syllabus, one that is especially interesting in advanced courses for specific purposes of various kinds.

There are several reasons why recommendations regarding the selection of teaching techniques to be used in any segment of a syllabus based on the proportional approach are outside the scope of the present work. One is that choice of specific techniques must be left in the hands of the syllabus designer and teachers involved in a particular situation, and ought not to be treated in detail except in the context of a given course or program. Provision for variety and for shifting the focus ought to be major concerns, together with some consideration of

Krashen's observations on the encouragement of language acquisition rather than language learning.[4]

It would be a reasonable approach to teach the linguistic system early, and to teach it all along in varying degrees, but also to enrich the teaching program with other components of communicative competence. What these components are, and how one accomplishes this enrichment through the design of an appropriate syllabus have been the two main themes of the present work. The notion of balance and of proportion is central in both themes as it is in discussing questions of methodology. In examining the enormous variety of classroom techniques which are available to the teacher, it is apparent that they too reflect the continuum on which communicative syllabus types can be ranged, and choices have to be made at the level of implementation which are consistent with the overall approach adopted.

The matter is complicated. There are a great many structural teaching materials representing various schools of thought, from grammar-translation to audio-lingual and audio-visual. There is also a range of more 'functional' materials, as well as a number of very original teaching techniques which may be labelled 'communicative', which the practising teacher may use to create his own materials. There is also the notion of the basic communicative unit, and allied to it ways of exploiting 'authentic' material.

Littlewood (1978) provides a convenient framework for looking at the question of methodology when he identifies three fields that are currently being explored in the search for an approach appropriate to the communicative approach. There has already been some debate about which of the three is most legitimate.

Retain Old Techniques

The first is simply to retain old techniques, but to adapt them to reflect the functional component of meaning more clearly. This is a widely adopted position, familiar by now to North American readers who have read Paulston and Bruder (1976), Finocchiaro (1978), Dobson (1979) and others. Dialogues and drills are both still used extensively, but the focus is at least partially on function as well as on form, in that the language is more realistic. An example might be:

Declining Invitations

Your friend wants you to go out with him, but you prefer to remain at home.

Friend: Would you like to go to a show?
You: No thanks, I don't feel like a show.
Friend: Would you prefer to go out for a snack?
You: No thanks, I don't feel like a snack.

The language is still controlled, though there can be scope for opening up the dialogue frame once the learners are confident enough to do so, and for providing instructions only about the general semantic content an utterance in a dialogue should have, leaving it to the learner to provide the actual linguistic focus or exponents.

New Teaching Techniques

The second possibility is to develop new teaching techniques. With this approach learners are given opportunities for language use in the classroom. The teacher tries to provide practice that will be more like communicative activity in the outside world, but the material is specially produced and content can be graded in various ways. The chief techniques now being employed are communication tasks and games, and simulations and role play. In the former, there are two basic principles: *information gap* among the learners themselves, and a *reason* for bridging the gap. In the latter, real-life situations are simulated and the learners assigned specific roles to play and goals to reach. There have been some volumes published which provide descriptions of communicative language teaching techniques (e.g. the British Council's ELT Guide No. 1, 1970; Holden, 1978; *RELC Journal* Supplement No. 1, 1979; Grellet, 1981) and there are an increasing number of articles in journals aimed at teachers which give advice on how to devise one's activities in such a way as to take into account the characteristics of one's own situation and that of one's students.

This approach fits in with Alexander's view of what the core of any course based on functional–notional principles must be: "*improvisation or transfer* in which students are invited to cope with real-life situations (*transaction* and *interaction*)." He goes on to point out that transfer may be simulated, as in communicative games, tasks, simulations and roleplays, or "real, in which students are invited to respond in their own persona" (Alexander, 1979, p.111). Improvisation or communicative activities can certainly be a problem in early stages of language teaching, as the teacher must be able to get the description of the situation or task across to the learners. (This is one additional reason for waiting a little in the proportional framework before introducing communicative work.) In all situations and at all levels, we may agree with Alexander when he expresses the opinion that the teacher may need considerable skill as a manager to conduct these activities successfully.

Communication as a Primary Technique

The third field of interest distinguished by Littlewood is of more recent origin. In it, we move completely outside the traditional framework of presentation, practice and free expression common to most methodologies. In this view, the answer to the question of what we are doing as language teachers is *not* that we are teaching language through communication, but that we are teaching communication through language. The focus is off language as such and no attempt can be made to present any aspect of the elements of communication in a systematic way. Teachers are by now familiar with various methods or approaches which have been developed (some quite outside applied linguistics and language teaching) to take account of the principle that what goes on in the classroom must be real, not simulated, interaction. Gattegno's *Silent Way,* Curran's *Community Language Learning,* Asher's *Total Physical Response,* Lozanov's *Suggestopedia* all exhibit a tendency toward communication as a primary technique. Experience in Canada with immersion teaching could be said to belong in this area too as there is no instruction in linguistic form at the early stage.

Sequencing vs. Continuity

There is a further school of thought (the best-known representatives of which are Christopher Candlin and Michael Breen of the University of Lancaster) which bases its arguments for a fully communicative approach to classroom teaching on the functional analysis of language and of meaning. Candlin (1976, p.250) writes:

The designer of language-learning materials cannot, therefore, hope to explain illocution in the precise way that he can explain grammatical focus; he can only conventionalize on the basis of par excellence examples at first selected on the grounds of their probability of this or that illocutionary interpretation in this or that event.

This view has profound implications for the sequencing or grading of the language data with which we wish to present our students. In Candlin's view, we should organize such data on a cline of increasing questionability of meaning, and in so doing change our teaching approach. This proposal reflects Candlin's experience in discourse analysis, and he makes it clear that a mere "item-bank of speech acts" cannot be said to constitute a syllabus, and points out that we must give to our learners not only the ability to recognize and produce appropriate speech acts but also that of managing a sentence. In so doing, the individual is communicating by the simultaneous realization in language of the ideational, interpersonal and textual systems. This is the nature of communication, and it should also be in the nature of language teaching.

For anyone making these assumptions, the syllabus type labelled "Fully Communicative" (our sixth category of communicative types) would have of necessity to be adopted. In it, sequencing "derives from the state of the learner(s) rather than from any implicit 'logic' of the content itself. 'Simplicity' and 'complexity', 'frequency' and 'infrequency' in any absolute sense cease to have any value in communicative methodology" (Candlin and Breen, 1979, p.198). For sequencing in the traditional sense Candlin and Breen substitute the concept of continuity. Continuity is possible from activity to activity, task to task. It also lies within communicative performance, and is provided through ideational knowledge. It resides, furthermore, in a "skill repertoire or cycle of skill-use during an activity or task" (Candlin and Breen, 1979, p.199). This concept embraces all three areas of meaning, and resembles Corder's remarks on cyclic sequencing referred to earlier. However, what is distinctive about this view is the insistence on the non-separability of the three components of meaning, and the rejection of any attempt to separate them during the teaching process.

A corollary of the views expressed by most of those working within the third field of methodological development in ESL is the necessity to work from authentic materials only. The use of contrived or specially prepared materials of any sort is rejected as theoretically unsound, given the unpredictable nature of human communication and the need to help the second-language learner along his way to true negotiation of meaning. There is at the present time a great deal of concern among some linguists with methodological aspects of communicative language teaching. Richterich (1979) has declared himself to be far more interested now in the learner's trajectory than in his target, and in an imaginative and inventive approach to pedagogy. We may expect, as suggested above, growing concern with the concept of autonomous or self-directed learning as well, which will overlap with interest in the exploitation of authentic material.

The syllabus designer working within a proportional approach will use materials from all three methodological camps. There is no reason at present to adopt only one or discard any of the possibilities, as long as they fit into the overall conception of a given syllabus. The level of a particular course, its purpose, its target criteria, the characteristics of the learners, the degree of preparation of the teacher—all of these factors will be taken into account when choices are being made. Rich variety and concern for the characteristics of *intake* should be guiding principles, and a certain amount of tracking will be required to ensure that a course is progressing within the framework suggested by the syllabus designer. But to adhere exclusively to one or other of the methodological alternatives would be unwise, and would impair both the flexibility and the balance of the proportional approach.

In an effort to combine all the strands of components of a communicative syllabus, as well as to provide the necessary variety of learning activities, the proportional model can be thought of as being three- rather than two-dimensional. Two of the dimensions will be the duration of the course, and true balance achieved among the components (as shown in Fig. 14), but the range of methodological techniques used to implement the syllabus will represent a third dimension. This third dimension can also be regarded as a stage subsequent to the preparation of the proto-syllabus, in other words as a pedagogical syllabus. But since decisions on all these aspects of course design are sometimes taken together, a three-dimensional rather than the two-stage version may represent more exactly the process of proportional syllabus design in many instances.

In both approaches, charts will be required for tracking. Jupp and Hodlin (1975), Finocchiaro (1979), and Alexander (1975) have provided charts which may serve as guides, and other examples appear in the appendices to the present work. It will be seen that these charts have the potential to inspire the production of a great deal of teaching material, given that the focus can be shifted from language to function to ideational content. Teaching and learning activities can also be varied extensively, any one of the combinations described being given a variety of treatments. This is one of the strengths of this approach and one which teachers appreciate the most, since the possibilities of combining material from various areas in different ways are almost inexhaustible.

Notes

1. Stratton (1977) considered that because second-language learning was a more conscious activity than acquiring one's mother tongue, it might be that the communicative syllabus makes demands that are too heavy in terms of the numbers of strands or components to be interrelated. But if one accepts Krashen's theories, the work of conscious interrelation of all the components belongs principally in the hands of the syllabus designer, not those of the learner (except in situations of total self-direction in which case the strands presumably need not all be identified as such).
2. I am indebted to my colleague, C. S. Jones, for suggesting the term.
3. Zobl (1980) discusses some of the research in untutored second-language acquisition; he argues that while natural language interaction does not exhibit a restriction on structural variety, this state of affairs does not obtain when one of the participants is a language learner.
4. In a definition of the term *intake,* Krashen characterizes it as "that input language that acquirers can actually utilize for language acqusition". He speculates that intake may have the following four characteristics: it is understood by the acquirer; it is slightly in advance of the acquirer's current stage of grammatical competence; it gets progressively more complex (though the optimal sequence is not obvious, and it is not possible to derive it from a linguistic description only): and it is natural communication (Krashen, 1978, p.22). See Krashen (forthcoming), for a discussion of the practical implications of this definition.

Chapter 8:

Designing a Communicative Syllabus: Stages IV and V

THE FINAL stages are now at hand. Returning to the description of Language Program Development, it can be seen that at the end of Stage III, the syllabus designer will know a good deal (although not always as much as he would wish) about the needs of the learners and the resources available with which to meet these needs. A decision about the type of communicative syllabus that will be most effective will also have been taken. Two major phases remain: the preparation of the proto-syllabus, and the elaboration of a pedagogical version of it.

Stage IV: The Proto-Syllabus

At this stage, the syllabus designer will turn to the description of the content that the syllabus will have, i.e., the preparation of syllabus specifications. As indicated above, in any communicative syllabus type it is likely that there will be a large number of components to be considered. These might include general notions and specific topics, communicative functions, discourse and rhetorical skills, variety of language, role-sets, and communicative events, as well as grammar and lexis. The work involved in selecting and combining items in each category is somewhat complicated, and it is far from familiar to teachers who are used to working from a structural syllabus. Accordingly, it is very useful to examine works such as *Threshold Level* and *Waystage,* since they are the classic examples of the notional–functional proto-syllabus. Although one might decide on a different number or alternative arrangement of the components of a communicative syllabus, much can be gained from an understanding of the Council of Europe documents.

In deciding how or even whether to account for all aspects of communicative competence, there are some considerations which the syllabus designer should bear in mind before beginning. First, it is not always either possible or desirable to include everything; much will depend on physical constraints involved in a given program, as well as convictions about syllabus type.[1] Some preliminary thought as to what is both desirable and possible may save considerable wear and tear on the syllabus designer, and assist in reducing the process to manageable porportions. Second, thought given at an early stage to describing the general purpose of the course (Stage II) will help in later decisions about syllabus type, which type in turn influences the arrangement of the syllabus specifications. Consideration of the amount and quality of information available from the needs survey will aid in determining how many components the syllabus should have, and later on how these should be related to each other. And third, the specification of target levels should be given early attention, since one should ask oneself whether it is realistic to specify these levels very closely if no correspondingly finely-tuned instruments are currently available with which to measure them.

Once some work has been carried out at this level, preferably in conjunction with other participants in the process (teachers, administrators, and learners too if possible), it is appropriate to start mapping out the syllabus content. This is usually done by working from inventories or lists, which are in a sense the basic tools of the syllabus designer. These inventories can be of various kinds. Some, like word frequency lists, have been drawn up after empirical research carried out on a corpus of language. Others, like the inventories of functions, were originally derived from work in philosophy of language. Others are simply dictionaries of various kinds. Still others, like lists of specific topics, would have to be created on the basis of a given needs analysis. (A list of some inventories which are available appears in Appendix I.)

A caveat is necessary here concerning the selection of lexis. While references to word frequency lists have been included, these are not always dependable sources of lexical items which will meet the criterion of appropriateness in any given course design. For beginning and intermediate levels in ESL both *Waystage* and *Threshold Level* are useful guides, but these works will always require modification to suit local conditions. For more advanced courses where closer integration with subject matter is required, the syllabus designer will need to wait for more information from the discourse analysts, and to rely on his own intuitions as well as locally–available information in selecting vocabulary items. He may also want to consult the numerous technical item-banks that exist as well as examining authentic samples of language (written and oral) of the kind the learner will be dealing with.

As far as the selection of linguistic forms is concerned, there are so many sources available, in the form of reference and pedagogical grammars, that there is no need to list them in detail. In specifying the other components of the syllabus (those that the new interest in communicative competence has produced), sets of checklists derived from the reference works indicated in the list of 'tools' (Appendix I) will prove to be very useful indeed. Teachers are already familiar with coping with the formal linguistic system through the use of pedagogical grammars. They cope with the semantic system through the choice of situations and themes. The most useful checklists are thus those related to components of the pragmatic aspects of the language system. Several categories can be provided for in these checklists: communicative functions, discourse skills and study skills. (A typical format appears in Appendix II.) It should be stressed once more that these are checklists, not questionnaires; they are guidelines *to be used by the syllabus designer,* not to be given to anyone else to 'fill out' in their raw form. Such sets of planning instruments may serve in various ways:

1. to make an initial definition of content for a projected program;
2. to map out a syllabus already being used;
3. to carry out 'retrospective mapping',[2] that is to record systematically what actually went on in a given course.

The last is often necessary, as in the communicative approach to language teaching a certain flexibility is necessary in order to achieve one's purpose. Some advance idea of what should be taught is essential, but it also sometimes necessary to reflect on what has actually taken place in contradistinction to what one projected would take place in the classroom. A projective or prospective mapping and a retrospective one can quite easily be compared. All of this work is simply a way of keeping a sensible check on what one is doing in the classroom, of 'managing' the various components of communicative competence in recognition of the fact that they exist, and of the fact that one has an obligation to teach them all.

Using Checklists to Specify Content

A series of checklists which can be used in preparing a syllabus appear in Appendix II. They were compiled from the sources indicated, and were developed in the light of experience gained in planning a variety of syllabuses in ESP, in working with teacher trainees who have contributed from their own rich experience of teaching situations, and in the preparation of syllabuses in other languages for groups of learners in professional settings in government and industry. The checklists include sections for communicative functions, discourse skills, and study skills. They have in all cases been supplemented or altered in various ways during development of the syllabus design for each project in which they were used. They have been field-tested in institutions other than that with which the writer is affiliated, and have served as aids in developing course materials appropriate to a number of different educational settings.[3] In some instances, questionnaires and worksheets based on the checklists resemble closely the lists for the needs survey; in others, specifications have been made directly from checklists as they stand, that is to say intuitively, or through interviews with learners without the use of questionnaires at all.

In addition to those which are included in the present work, a further checklist could be developed to cover Canale and Swain's 'strategic competence'. This they define as being made up of

> . . . verbal and non-verbal communication strategies that may be called into action to compensate for breakdowns in communication due to performance variables or to insufficient competence. Such strategies will be of two main types: those that relate primarily to grammatical competence (e.g. how to paraphrase grammatical forms that one has not mastered or cannot recall momentarily) and those that relate more to sociolinguistic competence (e.g. various role-playing strategies, how to address strangers when unsure of their social status) (Canale and Swain, 1980, pp.30–31).

However, as these authors comment, there has been very little work the area of these coping strategies, and it is premature to provide a taxonomy of them, let alone to suggest that they should be actively taught. Holec (1980a) refers to a similar group of strategies, which he labels *compensation* or *repair* strategies. Most of those he describes are covered in the checklist for discourse skills. They have been considered here as an integral part of skill in managing both written and oral language in the creation of text.

The short introduction to the checklists included in the appendices provides some informal comments concerning the details of their use. The selection of items from each area (including grammar and vocabulary) is likely to be a long process, and it should be viewed as something continuous. If one is working on the preparation of a totally new program of course one must expect to make use of subsequent feedback from the classroom to confirm or to modify the inclusion of a given item. If one is reorienting an existing curriculum, an examination of the content of the courses currently being taught is undertaken at this point. Items already included are noted (along with the material being used to teach them), and those that are not included are so identified. Plans are made to work them into the future design of the course under examination.

Some problems with this procedure will no doubt manifest themselves. For example, teacher-constructed syllabuses (as opposed to one being planned by the syllabus designer, whether he is acting independently of the teachers in the course, or whether he is in fact one of their number) will differ in format. Their variation in description and detail will also be complicating factors. The best rule of thumb to use in this process would seem to be that all information explicitly stated by the teacher should fit in somewhere. That is, the syllabus designer should try to include it all, even if the terms used by the teacher do not coincide with the ones he is using. It is really a problem of translation; there are likely to be instances in which the syllabus designer might read too much or too little into the teacher's work. One would hope that consultation with the teacher would solve this problem. A more difficult problem is likely to be 'translation' of structurally-oriented teacher-constructed syllabuses, and the problem of reliable breakdown in terms of language functions. However, this kind of mapping will serve to provide an initial picture of what is being covered in a course prior to reorientation, even though the picture may be incomplete or misinterpreted at some points.

Once the specifications are drawn up, there is a final stage to be gone through. Lists of items may be necessary, but they do not produce lesson plans. A list of functions, topics and linguistic exponents of functions must be considered the raw version of a communicative syllabus. A further step is necessary. The process of producing a *pedagogical* syllabus provides the teacher with material that has been to some extent predigested, and from which it is possible to procede more or less directly to classroom interaction.

Stage V: The Pedagogical Syllabus

It is with the pedagogical syllabus that some of the apparent difficulties surrounding early formulations of the functional approach can be resolved. The two main criticisms that have been directed at the Wilkins and van Ek formulations are that they ignore psycholinguistic considerations altogether, and that they lead to a phrase-book approach as far as methodology is concerned. This is not necessarily the case, however.

Let us look at the first objection. In order to develop communicative competence, it is now widely recognized that the psychology of the classroom is extremely important. (It is not necessary to reiterate the arguments already provided; the reader should however recall the work of Stevick and Krashen in particular.) In other words, psycholinguistic considerations are now thought to be more important in second-language teaching than the contributions of theoretical linguistics.

However, the wants, needs and desires of the learners are important aspects of the psychology of the classroom. One way of taking this aspect of the learner's psychology into account is through the provision of a needs-based yet flexible curriculum. The communicative syllabus provides this approach to second-language learning and teaching, as long as syllabus design is viewed as being a dynamic process, and not as having as its end the specification of a static list of items-to-be-learned. The components produced in the proto-syllabus stage are to be viewed as guidelines, not blueprints. They are organizing strategies. Room is left for further input once the syllabus is implemented, according to actual needs.

The presence of a syllabus in no way inhibits the creation of a comfortable classroom atmosphere. It is intended rather to provide the teacher with knowledge about the learner, the purposes he or she may have in learning English, and to match this knowledge with appropriate content and teaching techniques. Understanding the learning process and knowing when, where to contribute, and when—and how—to stand aside, is crucial for the successful teacher. This does not imply that the teacher must therefore go unprepared to class. Thus a form of pedagogical syllabus which can fill the teacher's needs without unduly circumscribing desirable classroom interaction can and must be provided.

The second objection which dates from a decade or so ago, has proven groundless, because the methodology which is now labelled 'communicative' is growing richer and richer. As long as the linguistic exponents of communicative functions set out in a proto-syllabus are never interpreted as being the equivalent of basic sentence patterns to be practised by rote, there is no need to be fearful that teaching will fall once more into a dull and repetetive routine.

The pedagogical syllabus provides a repertoire of words and phrases, chosen as exponents of functions and suitable to the topics identified as important to the learner. It is the teacher's role to make this repertoire come to life by choosing and carrying out communicative activities of a wide variety. Wilkins and van Ek of course were concerned with the process of constructing the linguistic repertoire, not with getting the learner to use it.

Forms of the Pedagogical Syllabus

What forms might a pedagogical syllabus take, and how best can it be structured so as to avoid the 'phrasebook' pitfall? Since this is the culminating phase of the syllabus design process, its realization will have to contain approaches to both teaching and learning, concerns which are essentially absent from Stage V. (It might also contain approaches to testing; but this complex area is not discussed here.[4]) The approaches taken will be influenced by decisions taken in Stage III. As there are various options available in syllabus types, so there are alternatives in the construction of or choice of format for a pedagogical syllabus.

A pedagogical syllabus for a Type 1 or 2 communicative syllabus would revolve around the choice of the unit of organization. As indicated in Chapter 6, such units can be given a functional, a notional or a structural focus. The production of a unit with a structural focus is entirely familiar to experienced teachers; the production of a unit with a functional or a notional one may not be. Alexander (1975) provides a complex grid which includes a cell for each of the following categories: functions; notions; settings and topics; social, sexual and psychological roles; style and range; grammar and lexis (Fig. 16). This grid has inspired the production of a great number of basic units for oral work, usually with a situational application, and with emphasis on various functions. Generally, a central function is chosen for each unit, with subsidiary ones to support it. The functions thus chosen are matched to a general situation and to specific topics. The units are then filled out, often in the form of a role-play or dialogue, and the language forms and vocabulary are drawn from the plot or scenario that results. A typical procedure might be as follows.

A BASIC UNIT

(Production of a partial unit in communicative work, in a syllabus in English for social purposes.)

(A)   *Situation or Event:* Shopping
       Central Functions: Agreeing/Disagreeing

Activity 1.1 Picking up your friend. (P = Productive requirement; R = Receptive requirement.)

Functions	*Tone* (appropriate to role; will influence choice of exponent)
1.1.1 Greeting (P)	Pleasant
1.1.2 Suggesting (P)	Intimate, pleasant
1.1.3 Disagreeing (P)	Patient, polite
1.1.4 Agreeing (P)	Neutral or Flattering
Repeat 1.1.2 to 1.1.4 as required.	Add in attention signals.
1.1.5 Telling	Intimate
1.1.6 Questioning	Curious
1.1.7 Responding	Excited

Activity 1.2 Entering Store

1.2.1 Requesting (P)	Courteous

1.2.2 Giving information (R)	Courteous
1.2.3 Thanking (P)	Courteous

Activity 1.3 Choosing a garment

1.3.1 Requesting (P)	Courteous
1.3.2 Giving information (R)	Courteous
1.3.3 Persuasion (R)	Insistent
1.3.4 Hesitation (P)	Defensive
1.3.5 Persuasion (R)	Flattering, insistent
1.3.6 Disagreeing (P)	Annoyed
1.3.7 Agreeing (R)	Polite
1.3.8 Leave-taking (P)	Abrupt

(B) *Exponents:* (for 1.1.1 to 1.1.4 only—exponents for the other functions could of course be listed in the same way.)

Activity 1.1 Picking up your friend.

1.1.1 Hello, Hi
Lovely morning, isn't it?
You look great today!

1.1.2 I thought we'd start at
Let's start at . . .   )
Why don't we start at . . .   )   Smith's, then go on to
Would you like to start . . .)   Jones'
What about starting at . . .)

1.1.3 Do you think we'll have enough time?
Perhaps we should *begin* at   )
Couldn't we begin at . . .   )   Jones'
I think it might be better if we began at)

1.1.4 O.K. by me
Sure, why not?
I don't mind
You're quite right.
Let's do that.

(C) *Making a lesson plan from the basic unit:*
1. Provide students with exponents. Rehearse and discuss.
2. Communicative activities:
   a) directed role play
   b) 'free' role-play (students to create interaction).
   c) production of written account of the event.

General functional categories	Notions: general and specific	Settings and topics	Social, sexual and psychological roles	Style and range*	Grammar and lexis
Language acts operating through	What?	Where?	Who?	How?	With what means?
1. Factual 2. Intellectual 3. Emotional 4. Moral 5. Suasive 6. Social Two types of exponents: 1. Fixed phrases 2. 'Grammatical system'	Often abstract: appropriate to a large variety of topics and situations	Concrete transaction	Friends	Style:	As they arise in each situation
			Strangers	formal	
	Directly determined by the choice of topic	General open-ended conversation or argument	Officials etc.	informal Range: 'cline': certain tentative uncertain	
EXAMPLES:					
1. Inquiring about	the availability of tickets	Concrete: box office	Stranger/Official	Formal	As in example
Are there	any tickets for tonight's performance?				
2. Inquiring about	the existence of theatres	General	Friend/Friend		As in example
Are there	any good theatres in your area?				

* Less applicable at Waystage,

Fig. 16. The Alexander Grid (Alexander, 1975).

A unit with a notional bias would resemble the functional one but give more prominence to the topics than to the functions. Such units do in fact resemble the old-fashioned phrase book, since they must supply a good deal of material associated with topics rather than starting from an essentially non-language-specific basis.

In realizing syllabus types 1 and 2, the pedagogical syllabus would consist of a number of these functional units, of greater or lesser complexity. That is, they might or might not contain elements from all of Alexander's cells. They might contain elements from a list of rhetorical or text skills or study skills as well for the purposes of work with written language. Several ESP and EST textbooks have been designed to include such elements.[5] Depending upon the degree to which structural units are to be present and the importance they have in the syllabus design, functional units might be 'grafted on' to the structural ones and reflect and recycle items already treated structurally. In some cases, there is simply an alternating emphasis throughout a given course. In Syllabus Type 3, the variability appears from level to level within a long-term language program, rather than from unit to unit within a level or course.

Syllabus Type 4, the functional variety, would call for the exclusive use of functional units, to the exclusion of any linguistic or structural ones. Type 5, the fully notional syllabus, would require a pedagogical syllabus which carefully specified the notions and topics to be included along with the functions, although the form of the basic unit might be the same as for the functional syllabus. Type 6 would of course require no pedagogical syllabus at all, but rely on the learner to provide a syllabus to the teacher through examination of the skills and knowledge he brings with him to the classroom, as well as through expression of his needs. And finally there is the task-based syllabus which is constructed along entirely different principles from those outlined here, is non-linguistic in nature and so outside the scope of this work (see Johnson, 1982, for discussion.)

What we have discussed so far is the elaboration of a new kind of 'basic unit' or lesson, and how it may be related to existing techniques for the construction of structural units or lessons. Functional, notional and situational units are already being used as the basis for ESL textbooks. Many of them are based on a generalized perception of what the learner's initial needs in learning English will be, and could be used in EFL situations with additional input from the teacher wherever possible. Some are geared towards the needs of the student in ESP or EAP courses in English-speaking countries. Most tend to be somewhat repetitious, since their authors, once having decided on a 'basic unit', then produce a number of units all cut from the same pattern.

The Pedagogical Syllabus as Handbook

There is another possibility which provides much more variety and flexibility. It is to realize the proto-syllabus as a handbook, addressed either to the teacher alone, or for many teaching contexts, to both teacher and learner. Working from lists of situations, topics, functions and their exponents, and so on, the syllabus designer will break the lists up into sections or chunks, and by fitting chunks from each list together, will produce a series of units. Three units however, will *not* be translated into a dialogue or role play or other specified classroom activity or interactional task. Instead, a selection of suitable activities and tasks will be provided. The exact manner in which items from each chunk are to be drawn together into a lesson plan, or translated into communicative interaction in the classroom, is left to the teacher. Better yet, whenever it is possible to do so, it ought to be a matter for negotiation between the teacher and the learners. Not *all* the material in each unit needs to be used each time; instead, a variety of combinations is possible, and a single unit can serve to inspire a large number of activities and tasks over a number of days or weeks. With the aid of such a handbook, the teacher can ensure that there is a spiral approach to sequencing of topics, functions and forms, since a single unit can be treated repeatedly, or 'revisited'. A unit for such a handbook might be set forth as follows:

(A) *Situation or Event:* Shopping
     Central Functions: Agreeing/Disagreeing.
     The aim of this unit is to provide you with the ability to manage a conversation (a) with a friend about where to shop, and (b) with a sales clerk about what to buy.

(B)   *Language you will need*

1.1   (a) With your friend:

1.1.1   I thought we'd start at
Let's start at . . .   )
Why don't we start at . . .   )   Smith's then go on to
Would you like to start at . . .)   Jones'
What about starting at . . .   )

1.1.2   Do you think we'll have enough time?
Perhaps we should *begin* at   )
Couldn't we begin at . . .   )   Jones'
It think it might be better if we began at)

1.1.3   O.K.
Sure, why not?
I don't mind
You're quite right.
Let's do that.

1.2   (b) With the sales clerk

1.2.1   I'd like (to buy) a . . .
Where can I find a . . .
Where are the . . .
On what floor   )   are the . . .
In which department   )

1.2.2   Can you help me, please?
Are you free just now?
Are you busy?

1.2.3   What size is this?
Are you sure this is a (size) X?
Do you have a (size) X?
Do you have a larger/smaller size?

1.2.4.   I do not think it fits well.
I don't like the fit.
It doesn't suit me.
I don't think I like it.

1.2.5.   It won't do at all.
I do not want it.
It just does not fit me.

(C) *Activities or Tasks:*

  1. Review appropriate vocabulary: names of articles of clothing, colours, numbers, etc.
  2. Using a catalogue, make up a shopping list. Specify the kind of articles you need in some detail, e.g. 'A light blue blouse with short sleeves, size 10, not just 'a blue blouse'.
  3. Telephone three stores to ask whether they have what you need.
  4. Role-play: Ask your teacher to be the salesperson; he or she should try to sell you something you do not want. Try using various expressions to convey your wishes.
  5. Go to a store and try to buy or to get information about the items you want.
  6. Write a letter to your teacher, telling how your shopping trip was. Did you get what you wanted?

This is a very simple unit, of course. The content is restricted and the forms are not very numerous. The teacher (or the materials writer) could fill out such a unit with reference to all the properties that items the learner was interested in might have. The type of anticipated inter-action can also be extended greatly, depending upon the items and the contexts involved. This type of unit could be used to encourage skill in using both oral and written forms of English, by providing a large number of pre-and post-lesson activities. Selections would be made, both from the list of exponents and from the list of activities, according to particular classroom constraints.

Implications for the Classroom

The most obvious effect of using a syllabus set out in this way would be a significant change in the role of the teacher. In teaching adults and in attempting to negotiate with them about the process, it is evident that the teacher abandons the position of authority figure and becomes a guide rather than a leader, or even the learners' peer. That this alter-ation in role is in line with current views of the psychology of language learning is plain enough. It also implies, however, an equally radical change in the learner, who would be expected to assume a much more active status in a far more active process. In order to achieve this altered balance in the classroom, both teacher and learner need to know more about what they are undertaking.

In order to be successful the teacher quite evidently must accept that his position will be far less central than before. To do this he must accept current theories of second-language acquisition, and be prepared to use a strategy which is rather different from the one traditionally associated with second-language teaching. The syllabus provided will depend for success on having teachers available who understand why the items in it have been selected, why a communicative methodology is essential, what this methodology consists of, and how to implement and encourage the communicative activities suggested. The best and most successful will be able to create a larger range of activities based on their own knowledge and experience as well as on the learners' characteristics.

Moreover, in order for the learner to accept the use of a communicative handbook rather than a structural textbook, some re-education will have to take place. The learner will need to know a lot more about communicative language teaching than is usual at present. This takes time, and there are cases in which a dose of structural medicine is necessary from time to time to keep things moving. Particularly if methodology leans away from anything which is obviously linguistic and tilts toward the more clearly semantic tasks and activities, the learner must understand that using language for communicative purposes is the most efficient way of acquiring linguistic structures.

The whole procedure of communicative syllabus design is still in an early stage. To obtain good results from a communicative handbook such as the one described here, it will not be enough simply to replace existing texts with new ones produced in the latest fashion. Communicative language teaching requires good teacher preparation and an active contribution from the learner. Furthermore, in order to assess the directions in which language teaching is moving, new procedures for comparative evaluation of language programs will be required. As it is difficult if not impossible to compare programs with differing aims and objectives, it is probably going to be necessary to establish consensus on some broad groupings along the lines proposed in Chapter 6, with special attention to the socio-cultural features present in the environment.

Information Networks

To increase the possibilities for producing communicative syllabuses the use of information networks will be invaluable in providing access to banks of communicative activities and tasks. Methodology used in communicative language teaching is becoming increasingly more valid and rich. If the syllabus designer and the teacher are to use the large number of techniques that now exist it will be necessary to depend on taxonomies of such techniques and on item banks. Documentation centers will need to create cross-referencing systems designed to identify rapidly activities which will correspond in an appropriate manner to a large number of variables such as the learners' age, proficiency level, interests, and aims, as well as the topics, functions, focus, etc. of the course, and whether oral or written language is practised (or some proportion of each). Candlin (1981) has produced an exercise typology for the communicative teaching of English; Grellet (1981) has written one for reading comprehension exercise types; and both authors provide examples of each exercise type. Work with taxonomies such as these will be required in order to build up banks of items, and thus reduce the load on both the writer of pedagogical syllabuses and the classroom teacher.

The end result will be a series of sourcebooks or handbooks which should respond to concerns about the provision of a suitable classroom atmosphere, in that maximum variety and flexibility will be possible if they are properly used. They should also incorporate enough socio-cultural material to ensure that the sociolinguistic dimensions of communicative competence are looked after. And there is no reason to suppose that the purely linguistic skills will not also be catered to, depending upon decisions regarding syllabus type. All these concerns can be brought together in the pedagogical syllabus, and dealt with according to the requirements of specific programs. It is to be expected that the implementation of careful communicative syllabus design and the production of appropriate pedagogical syllabuses will turn out to be more valuable—and certainly more viable in the majority of cases—than the use of structural methods or of no syllabus at all. Finally, this approach to the solution of the problem of course design in second-language teaching is consistent with current psycholinguistic and sociolinguistic theories.

Notes

1. Munby states that a number of variables, which are constraints upon the implementation of the syllabus specifications, belong to a dimension of course design which is *subsequent* to syllabus specification. These variables are 1. socio-political, 2. logistical, 3. administrative, 4. psycho-pedagogical and 5. methodological (Munby, 1978, p.127). It would seem rather that it would be well to consider some of these *prior* to syllabus specification (2 and 3 for example) and others (4 and 5) concurrently with it. That it is unwise if not impossible to ignore the socio-political constraints of the day need hardly be said at all.
2. 'Retrospective' and 'prospective' mapping are terms which were used by Christopher Candlin in a presentation at TESOL, 1980, in San Francisco. I have not seen these terms used elsewhere.
3. Some of the ESP syllabuses thus produced have been reported on in Yalden (1980). Further reports will be forthcoming.
4. See B. Carroll (1980), and Morrow (1977) for discussion of the difficulties involved.
5. For example, the *English in Focus* series (Oxford University Press), and the *Reading and Thinking in English* series (Oxford University Press).

Conclusion

THE STAGES of syllabus design which are outlined in this work exhibit characteristics which separate the process of language program design quite sharply from that of the implementation of a language-teaching method. These differences have been treated in the course of the discussion above. The learner-centered aspect of the communicative syllabus is obviously important, as well as the large increase in the number of variables that will dictate the choice of syllabus type. Each teaching situation has the potential to generate a different set of syllabus specifications, and even these will need to be viewed as flexible and non-constraining—as suggestive, not as binding.

Flexibility and freedom appeal to some, but not to all. The inexperienced classroom teacher is often much happier with a predetermined 'method' in which everything is cut-and-dried. Most experienced teachers, however, prefer both freedom and responsibility, and so have shied away from methods too rigidly prescribed. The process of communicative syllabus design yields highly personalized teaching programs, which give both the learner and the teacher an optimal environment in which to work. However, the position of the individual responsible for the design of the syllabus has to be recognized as an integral part of the design and implementation of second-language teaching programs. Some initial planning is necessary; the teacher is not to be expected to step into the classroom unaided, any more than he would have entered a structurally-oriented classroom without texts and audio-visual apparatus.

But the situation today is more complex, as we move in a learner-centered direction. Time required for syllabus design should be set apart, and someone assigned the job of producing the necessary frameworks for teaching and learning. Such new requirements do not end with the production of the syllabus since the role of the syllabus designer is an ongoing one. As feedback from a set of specifications becomes available, he will be needed to assess the manner and degree of alteration necessary to the syllabus. Nor is the role of the teacher any less complicated simply because it is no longer the textbook which dictates what is to be done in class. On the contrary, the teacher's role requires fairly radical reorientation away from that of director or leader to that of monitor and even of peer. Furthermore, the culminating requirements in communicative language teaching are the teacher's ability to use the target language at native or native-like levels, to create materials and to stimulate interaction.

The demands on teachers will be great and it is therefore incumbent upon those who train them to do their best to ensure adequate exposure to both the theoretical and the practical bases of second-language pedagogy, including some knowledge of syllabus design theory. The matter of the degree of independence of the teacher is an important one and will require more thought. He should be both independent enough to create materials at least to fill in gaps in a syllabus, yet accepting of the overall concept which the syllabus designer has given him—a problem which arises in any instance when the roles of teacher or syllabus designer are not filled by the same person.

Teachers' attitudes to the concept of needs-based communicative syllabus design are therefore very important, especially if they are to work cooperatively and fruitfully as part of a team. They will have to accept the needs analysis (however it may be arrived at) and not be prescriptive in the usual sense about the kind of language they teach. In any attempt at fully communicative work, they will also have to accept the role of collaborator with their students, as the latter must be allowed to experiment and to participate, to a greater or lesser extent, in the learning–teaching process.

The question of the degree to which communicative language teaching will depend on the skill of the teacher in exploiting authentic material also needs further exploration. The whole matter of how much teaching material can be preserved and how much is essentially ephemeral remains something of a problem. In this respect, the sheer volume of work connected with the exploitation of authentic material may turn out to be disheartening, unless a means can be found to set up networks of language-teaching resource centers and to establish categories which will make for a reasonably efficient retrieval system. The amount of energy expended on creating materials will be better used when institutions find a way of indexing and storing materials which members of their staff create.

These are all questions to be dealt with in preparing teachers to work within a communicative framework. They are also questions to be considered by those responsible for second-language teaching programs at various levels, since they imply changed attitudes to the specification of goals and to anticipated outcomes, to the path to be taken toward such goals, and to the means which can be made available to learners and teachers alike. Finally, it is perhaps the most striking aspect of communicative language teaching that one is able to carry on discussions about it to a very large degree without talking solely about linguistic form. The subject matter is no longer what has traditionally been thought of as language as such. It is time to learn to use the new vocabulary.

Appendix I:

The Tools of the Syllabus Designer

THE SYLLABUS designer will require references for the following areas. Some examples of widely applicable works are given.

1. Communicative Functions

Leech, G. and Svartvik, J. (1975) *A Communicative Grammar of English*. Longman.
Munby, J. (1978) *Communicative Syllabus Design*. Cambridge University Press.
van Ek, J. (1975, 1980) *The Threshold Level*. Strasbourg: CCC, Council of Europe, 1975, and Pergamon, 1980.
van Ek, J. (1976) *The Threshold Level for Modern Language Learning in Schools*. London: Longman.
Wilkins, D. (1976) *Notional Syllabuses*. London: Oxford University Press.

2. Settings and Topics

These are best drawn from the forecast of the learner's needs. However, in order to assist in structuring information which may be coming in from a variety of sources, the syllabus designer can usefully consult *Threshold Level* or *Waystage*.

A useful work listing a variety of settings together with some appropriate linguistic exponents is Liz Baines *et al., Situations and Aids for Teaching Situations* (London: International House, 1976).

3. Lexis

Frequency lists may be helpful, but should be studied carefully before use, as the corpus and/or principles on which a given word frequency list is based may not be appropriate to a particular syllabus problem. Scientific and technical vocabularies, and dictionaries as required may be consulted.

Specialized dictionaries will often be useful. Some of the newer ones are: Longman's *Dictionary of English Idioms, Dictionary of Scientific*

Usage, and *Lexicon of Contemporary English.* The last of these has two sections which reflect the categories of the notional syllabus: Feelings, Emotions and Sensations; and Thought and Communication, Language and Grammar.

Pictorial dictionaries may also be helpful, e.g. *The English Duden,* compiled by Konrad Duden, Mannheim: Bibliographisches Institut, 1960.

4. Structures

a) In addition to the usual teaching grammars, a list of structures can be extremely useful. As well, Quirk and Greenbaum's grammar is an invaluable tool. *Threshold Level* and *Waystage* should be consulted as examples of how linguistic exponents are selected and then related to topics.

Alexander, L. G., Allen, W. S., Close, R. A. and O'Neill, R. J. (1975) *English Grammatical Structure.* A general syllabus for teachers. London: Longman.
Leech, G. and Svartvik, J. (1975) *A Communicative Grammar of English.* Longman.
Quirk, R. and Greenbaum, S. (1973) *A University Grammar of English.* Longman.

b) Some reference works on English word formation should be available to the syllabus designer as well as to the materials writer (e.g. V. Adams, *An Introduction to Modern English Word Formation,* London: Longman Group Ltd., 1973 and the Quirk and Greenbaum grammar, as it contains an Appendix on word formation, pp.973–1032).

5. Phonology/graphology

Manuals in these areas are necessary if a syllabus is to include attention to what Halliday called the substance of spoken and written language. *Threshold Level* contains no information in these areas. The syllabus designer will require at least some practical manuals such as Prator and Robinett's *Manual of American English Pronunciation* (New York: IIolt Rinehait, 1972), or Bowen's *Patterns of English Pronunciation* (Rowley, MA: Newbury House, 1975). There are also many textbooks available which contain practical exercises. This component of any syllabus is not directly related to learner's needs, and so can be handled conventionally as necessary.

6. Discourse and Rhetorical Skills

Munby's *Communicative Syllabus Design* includes a very detailed taxonomy of language skills, some of which are particularly related to discourse. There are no other taxonomies as such, except insofar as work in discourse and rhetorical analysis requires the establishment of categories. Universal agreement on terminology in this field is far from being achieved. I can therefore only refer the reader to certain key works and suggest that perusal of some of these will provide what is needed to make a start in characterizing such skills. It should be noted that materials writers sometimes include as 'study skills' some abilities that may be alternatively treated as discourse and/or rhetorical skills.

Discourse skills:

Coulthard, M. (1977) *An Introduction to Discourse Analysis.* London: Longman.
Sinclair, J. M., and Coulthard, M. (1975) *Towards an Analysis of Discourse: The English used by Teachers and Pupils.* London: Oxford University Press.
Larsen-Freeman, D. (1980) *Discourse Analysis in Second-Language Research.* Rowley, MA. Newbury House.

Rhetorical skills: (these references, while principally directed toward EST needs, nonetheless illustrate what this component of a syllabus might contain.)

Lackstrom, J., Selinker, L. and Trimble, L. P. (1970) "Grammar and technical English." in Lugton, (ed.) *English as a Second Language: Current Issues.* Philadelphia: The Center for Curriculum Development.
Lackstrom, J., Selinker, L. and Trimble, L. (1973) "Technical rhetorical principles and grammatical choice." *Tesol Quarterly,* 7, 127–33.
Mackay, R. (1979) "Teaching the information-gathering skills." In Mackay, Barkman and Jordan, (eds), *Reading in a Second-Language.* Rowley, MA: Newbury House.
Selinker, L., Todd-Trimble, M. and Trimble, L. (1978) "Rhetorical function, shifts in EST discourse." *Tesol Quarterly,* 12, 311–320.
Selinker, L., Todd-Trimble, R. M. and Trimble, L. (1976) "Presuppositional rhetorical information in EST discourse." *Tesol Quarterly,* 10, 281–90 (Note especially the diagram on p.283).
Widdowson, H. G. (1974) "An Approach to the teaching of scientific English discourse." *RELC Journal,* 5/1, 27–40.

Appendix II:

Syllabus Design Checklists

THIS appendix contains two sets of planning instruments, designed to be used in three ways:

1. in mapping a projected syllabus
2. in monitoring a syllabus in use
3. in retrospective mapping of a syllabus

PART A contains the Communications Needs Survey Checklists:

1. Purpose and Setting
2. Interaction and Instrumentality
3. Course Design Constraints

PART B contains the Syllabus Specifications Checklists:

1. Language functions
2. Discourse and Rhetorical Skills
3. Study Skills

The first set of checklists is designed to help the syllabus designer gather data about students, their characteristics and language background, their communication needs in the target language, and to specify some objectives for them. It will also assist in examining the teaching situation in which the syllabus will be used. The second set of checklists is to be used after the description of purpose is completed.

These checklists are not questionnaires; they are guidelines and are intended to be used to organize an approach to planning a communicative language program. They should guide the syllabus designer to obtain information needed to be able to write up a description of the purpose of a language program in terms of the learners' characteristics and needs. *These checklists are neither definitive nor exhaustive.*

They are included here as illustrations of what can be drawn up for a particular language program, working from existing models and taking into account local conditions.

The list of the communicative functions of language (Part B, I) derives from Wilkins' three-part division into ideational, modal and communicative meaning; however, I have conflated his 'modal' and 'communicative' levels, more along the lines of van Ek's model, and placed formulaic or phatic meaning into a separate category. The Discourse Skills Checklist (B, II) has been worked out from Munby (1978), Mackay (1979), and Mackay and Mountford (1976, 1978). Sections 1 and 2 ('Rhetorical Cohesion' and 'Interpreting the Text by Going Outside It') evidently owe much also to Halliday and Hasan (1976). Sections 3 and 4 ('Operations on a Text' and 'Rhetorical Organization of Discourse') are based on Munby (1978) and Mackay (1979), and also on Widdowson (1978) and Allen and Widdowson (1974), as well as from the practical experience gained by L. Young in the application of an earlier version of this list, and communicated informally to the writer. Section 5 is based on Munby, but rearranged in categories designed to reflect more clearly current work in discourse theory (e.g. Sinclair and Coulthard, 1975; Coulthard, 1977).

Checklist III in Part B, labelled Study Skills, includes components that have been developed primarily for programs for academic purposes (see Allen and Widdowson, 1974; Widdowson, 1978; Mackay, Barkman and Jordan, 1979). This section verges on methodological questions, but is included because it has been especially useful in preparing materials for teaching the written language, and helps to develop skills which are often lacking in college-age students.

PART A: Communication Needs Survey

Checklist I: Purpose and Setting
0.0 The learners
   0.1   *Identity*
   0.1.1 Age range _____
   0.1.2 Sex _____
   0.1.3 Nationality/ies _____
   0.1.4 Place of residence _____

0.1.5   Total number _____

0.2   *Language*

0.2.1   Mother tongue (L1) _____

0.2.2   Target language (L2) _____

0.2.3   Present level of the TL
- [ ] zero
- [ ] false beginner
- [ ] elementary
- [ ] low intermediate
- [ ] high intermediate
- [ ] advanced

1.0 Purpose for which target language is required

1.1   *Classification*

1.1.1   [ ] Occupational: pre- or post-experience

1.1.2   [ ] Educational: discipline—or school subject

1.1.3   [ ] General Interest

If you have checked: *1.1.1 Occupational,* fill in: 1.2 only

If you have checked: *1.1.2 Educational:* fill in: 1.3 only

If you have checked: *1.1.3 General Interest:* fill in: 1.4 only

1.2   *Occupational classification*

1.2.1   Type of worker
- [ ] manual
- [ ] clerical
- [ ] technical
- [ ] managerial
- [ ] professional
- [ ] officer
- [ ] creative artist/athlete

1.2.2   Field of Work
- [ ] commerce/industry
- [ ] public administration
- [ ] profession (medicine, law, teaching, etc.)
- [ ] science
- [ ] armed forces
- [ ] entertainment/arts
- [ ] utilities/services
- [ ] other _____

1.2.3   Specific occupation _____
_____

1.2.3.1 Central duty (where applicable) _____
_____

1.2.3.2 Other duties involving L2 _____
_____

1.3   *Educational purpose:*
1.3.1   Academic discipline classification
         ☐   mathematics
         ☐   physical science   ˎ
         ☐   humanities
         ☐   social science
         ☐   biological science
         ☐   medicine
         ☐   education
         ☐   engineering
         ☐   other _____
1.3.2   Specific discipline _____
1.3.3   Central area of study _____
1.3.4   Other areas of study _____
1.4   *General interest:*
         ☐   entertainment at home (radio, TV)
         ☐   entertainment at the theatre
         ☐   social activities (parties, gatherings)
         ☐   talking to friends
         ☐   community activities_____
         ☐   cultural interest _____
         ☐   reading books (What kind?) _____
         ☐   travel
         ☐   other needs_____

2.0 Setting.
   2.1   *Locations:*
   2.1.1   Cities, towns _____
   2.1.2   Place of work _____
   2.1.3   Place of study _____
   2.1.3.1 Level _____

2.1.3.2 Academic settings:
    ☐ lecture room
    ☐ classroom
    ☐ laboratory/workshop
    ☐ seminar/tutorial
    ☐ private study, library

2.1.4 Other places _____

2.1.5 Extent of use (international, national, local) _____

2.2 *Times*

2.2.1 What time of day is the L2 most required? _____

2.2.2 For how many hours per day/week is the L2 required?

    _____

2.2.2 Is the L2 required
    ☐ regularly
    ☐ often
    ☐ occasionally
    ☐ seldom

Checklist II: Interaction and Instrumentality

3.0 Interaction

3.1 *Position* _____

3.2 *Role set* (persons with whom learners will interact by virtue of their position)

    _____

4.0 Instrumentality

4.1 *Medium*
    ☐ Spoken: receptive
    ☐ Spoken: productive
    ☐ Written: receptive
    ☐ Written: productive

4.2 *Mode*
Detailed specification only required for a syllabus for a highly specific situation. Otherwise, two broad categories suffice:
    ☐ dialogue, spoken to be heard
    ☐ dialogue, written to be read

4.3   *Channel*
4.3.1   Bilateral (interactive)
☐   face to face
☐   telephone
☐   radio contact
☐   print
4.3.2   Unilateral
☐   face to face
☐   PA system
☐   radio
☐   TV
☐   recording
☐   film
☐   print

Checklist III: Course Design Constraints

5.0   The school or institution
5.1   *Level*
☐   Elementary
☐   Secondary
☐   Tertiary
☐   Other (adult education, government training institution, etc.)
5.2   *Sector*
☐   Private school
☐   Publicly funded school
☐   Government funded school
☐   Business-owned school

6.0   The teaching staff
6.1   *Total number* _____
6.2   *Teachers' qualifications and experience* _____
_____

7.0   Equipment available
☐   Tape recorders
☐   Overhead projectors
☐   Filmstrip projectors
☐   Film projectors

☐ Full language lab
☐ Duplicating service
☐ Other

8.0 Class size and timetabling
8.1   *Average number of pupils per class* _____
8.2   *Hours per week of instruction* _____
8.2.1   In class_____
8.2.2   In lab _____
8.3   *Construction of the timetable* (provide details)

PART B: Syllabus Specification Checklists

Checklist I: Language Functions

(A) Expressing truth values (ideational meaning)
1.   *Factual information*
1.1   identifying
1.2   reporting through description
1.3   reporting through narration
1.4   correcting
2.   *Argument*
2.1   expressing agreement/disagreement
2.2   confirmation/denial
3.   *Likelihood*
3.1   expressing possibility/impossibility
3.2   expressing probability/improbability
3.3   expressing logical conclusions (deduction)
3.4   expressing prediction and predictability
4.   *Attitudes to truth*
4.1   positive: expressing certainty/uncertainty
4.2   intermediate: expressing conjecture
4.3   weak: expressing doubt
4.4   negative: expressing disbelief
5.   *Seeking information*
5.1   questioning, inquiring

(B) Expressing mood, emotion and attitude (modal meaning)
    6.   *Emotional and moral attitudes*
    6.1   expressing approval, liking, satisfaction
    6.2   expressing preference
    6.3   expressing disapproval, disliking, dissatisfaction
    6.4   expressing interest/lack of interest
    6.5   expressing hope
    6.6   expressing disappointment
    6.7   expressing surprise
    6.8   expressing worry, fear
    7.   *Volition*
    7.1   insisting
    7.2   expressing intention
    7.3   expressing want, wish, desire
    7.4   expressing willingness
    8.   *Commitment*
    8.1   granting/seeking permission
    8.2   expressing obligation
    8.3   expressing prohibition
    9.   *Suasion* (getting things done)
    9.1   expressing commands; instructing, directing
    9.2   expressing requests
    9.3   inviting
    9.4   suggesting a course of action
    9.5   advising
    9.6   warning
    9.7   promising
    9.8   threatening

(C) Formulaic communication (phatic meaning)
    10.   *Greetings*
    10.1   greetings
    10.2   farewells
    10.3   introductions
    10.4   beginning/ending letters
    10.5   seasons greetings
    10.6   toasts

11.   *Acknowledgement*
11.1 thanking, expressing gratitude
11.2 apologizing
11.3 expressing regret
11.4 expressing appreciation
12.   *Empathy*
12.1 congratulations
12.2 condolences
13.   *Attention signals*
13.1 vocatives

Checklist II: Discourse Skills
(A) Cohesion and reference
  Value *0.0 Cohesion of text*
☐ 0.1   Understanding and expressing relations between parts of a text through *lexical cohesion* devices of
☐ 0.1.1 repetition
☐ 0.1.2 synonymy
☐ 0.1.3 hyponymy
☐ 0.1.4 antithesis
☐ 0.1.5 apposition
☐ 0.1.6 lexical set/collocation
☐ 0.1.7 pro-forms/general words
  0.2   Understanding and expressing relations between parts of a text through *grammatical cohesion* devices of
☐ 0.2.1 reference (anaphoric and cataphoric)
☐ 0.2.2 comparison
☐ 0.2.3 substitution
☐ 0.2.4 ellipsis
  Value *1.0 Rhetorical cohesion.* Recognizing and using discourse markers to signal relationships of

		examples of markers
☐	1.1 *enumeration*	*examples of markers*
☐	1.1.1 listing	first, second
☐	1.1.2 time sequence	then, next, finally
☐	1.2 *addition* (conjunction)	(and)
☐	1.2.1 reinforcing	furthermore, in addition
☐	1.2.2 similarity	similarly, equally

☐	1.3	*logical sequence*	(so)
☐	1.3.1	introduction	now
☐	1.3.2	summarizing	overall, so far
☐	1.3.3	result, consequence	so, consequently
☐	1.3.4	deduction, induction	therefore, hence
☐	1.3.5	conclusion	to conclude, to sum up
☐	1.4	*apposition*	(or)
☐	1.4.1	explication	that is, in other words
☐	1.4.2	exemplification/ illustration	for example, for instance
☐	1.5	*contrast*	(but)
☐	1.5.1	substitution	that is, I mean
☐	1.5.2	replacement	alternatively
☐	1.5.3	antithesis	conversely, instead
☐	1.5.4	concession	anyway, however

Value 2.0 *Interpreting the text by going outside it*
- ☐ 2.1 using exophoric reference
- ☐ 2.2 reading between the lines
- ☐ 2.3 integrating data in the text with own experience or knowledge of the world

(B) Operations on a text

Value 3.0 *Extracting salient points to summarize.*
- ☐ 3.0.1 the whole text
- ☐ 3.0.2 a specific idea/topic in the text
- ☐ 3.0.3 the underlying idea or point of the text

3.1 Selective extraction of relevant points from a text, involving
- ☐ 3.1.1 the coordination of related information
- ☐ 3.1.2 the ordered rearrangement of contrasting items
- ☐ 3.1.3 the tabulation of information for comparison and contrast

3.2 Expanding salient/relevant points into summary of
- ☐ 3.2.1 the whole text
- ☐ 3.2.2 a specific idea/topic in the text

3.3 Reducing the text through rejecting redundant or irrelevant information and items, especially
- ☐ 3.3.1 omission of closed-system items (e.g. determiners)

☐   3.3.2 omission of repetition, circumlocution, digression, false starts

☐   3.3.3 compression of sentences or word groups

☐   3.3.4 compression of examples

☐   3.3.5 use of abbreviations

☐   3.3.6 use of symbols denoting relationships between states, processes, etc.

(C) Rhetorical organization of discourse

4.0 Planning and organizing information in expository language (especially presentation of reports, expounding an argument, evaluation of evidence), using *rhetorical*

Value   *functions,* especially:

☐   4.0.1 generalization

☐   4.0.2 definition

☐   4.0.3 classification

☐   4.0.4 description of substances and their properties

☐   4.0.5 description of processes and their stages

☐   4.0.6 formulation of hypotheses

4.1   Recording information (expressing/understanding equivalence of meaning)

☐   4.1.1 within the same style (e.g. paraphrasing to avoid repetition)

☐   4.1.2 across different styles (e.g. from technical to lay)

4.2   Distinguishing the main idea from supporting details by differentiating

☐   4.2.1 primary from secondary significance

☐   4.2.2 the whole from its parts

☐   4.2.3 a process from its stages

☐   4.2.4 category from exponent

☐   4.2.5 statement from example

☐   4.2.6 fact from opinion

☐   4.2.7 a proposition from its argument

(D) Overt transactional skills in spoken discourse

Value   5.0 Initiating in discourse:

☐   5.0.1 how to initiate the discourse (elicit, inform, direct, etc.)

☐ 5.0.2 how to introduce a new point (using verbal and vocal cues)

☐ 5.0.3 how to introduce a topic (using appropriate micro-function such as explanation, hypothesis, question)

5.1 Maintaining the discourse:

☐ 5.1.1 how to respond (acknowledge, reply, loop, agree, disagree, etc.)

☐ 5.1.2 how to continue (add, exemplify, justify, evaluate, etc.)

☐ 5.1.3 how to adapt, as result of feedback, especially in mid-utterance (amplify, omit, reformulate, etc.)

☐ 5.1.4 how to turn-take (interrupt, challenge, inquire, dove-tail, etc.)

☐ 5.1.5 how to mark time (stall, 'breathing space', formulae, etc.)

☐ *5.2 Terminating in discourse:*

☐ 5.2.1 how to mark boundaries in discourse (verbal and vocal cues)

☐ 5.2.2 how to come out of the discourse (excuse, concede, pass, etc.)

5.3 Identifying and indicating the main point or important information in a piece of discourse

☐ 5.3.1 vocal underlining (e.g. decreased speed, increased volume)

☐ 5.3.2 end-focus and end-weight

☐ 5.3.3 verbal cues (e.g. 'The point I want to make is. . .')

Checklist III: Study Skills

Value 0.0 Basic reference skills: understanding and use of:

☐ 0.1 graphic presentation, viz. headings, sub-headings, numbering, indentation, bold print, footnotes

☐ 0.2 table of contents and index

☐ 0.3 cross-referencing

☐ 0.4 card catalogue

☐ 0.5 phonetic transcription/diacritics

☐ 0.6 bibliography

☐ 0.7 dictionaries

1.0 Skimming to obtain
☐   1.1   the gist of the text
☐   1.2   a general impression of the text
2.0 Scanning to locate specifically required information on
☐   2.1   a single point
☐   2.2   more than one point
☐   2.3   a whole topic
3.0 Transcoding information presented in diagrammatic display, involving
☐   3.1   straight conversion of diagram/table/graph into speech/writing
☐   3.2   interpretation or comparison of diagrams/tables/graphs in speech/writing
4.0 Transcoding information in speech/writing to diagrammatic display, through
☐   4.1   completing a diagram/table/graph
☐   4.2   constructing one or more diagrams/tables/graphs
5.0 Note-taking skills
☐   5.1   completing note-frames
☐   5.2   deletions
☐   5.3   use of symbols
☐   5.4   use of diagrams

Appendix III:

Personal Data Sheet: EAP Program, Adult Learners (Prepared by Patricia Pappas)

PLEASE answer the following questions and fill in the blanks clearly and to the best of your ability. Please PRINT. Use an 'X' to mark the boxes. Your instructor will help you if you need her.

A. IDENTITY

Name _____

Sex _____Age _____

Nationality _____

Home town/city _____

Address in Ottawa _____

_____

Phone Number _____

Mother tongue _____

Other languages spoken_____

read _____

Marital Status ☐ married ☐ single ☐ other

    If married, is your spouse with you? ☐ Yes ☐ No

    If spouse is not with you, will he/she

    be joining you? ☐ Yes ☐ No

    Do you have children? ☐ Yes ☐ No

    If so, how many?_____

    Will they be joining you in Ottawa ☐ Yes ☐ No

B. PAST EDUCATION

Field of study:

    ☐ commerce/business

174

☐   public administration
☐   professional (teaching, medicine, law, etc.)
☐   science
☐   utilities, services
☐   other _____

University attended _____
Location _____
Number of years at this institution _____
Degrees/Diplomas awarded
    1._____ Date_____
    2._____ Date_____
Total years of post-secondary education _____
Courses taken *in major field of study*
    1. _____   6. _____
    2. _____   7. _____
    3. _____   8. _____
    4. _____   9. _____
    5. _____10. _____
How many (if any) of these courses were in English?_____

C. FUTURE EDUCATION (NON-ESL)

Academic Discipline Classification
    ☐   mathematics
    ☐   physical science
    ☐   humanities
    ☐   social science
    ☐   biological science
    ☐   medicine
    ☐   education
    ☐   engineering
    ☐   other
Describe briefly the area you plan to specialize in

_____
_____
_____
_____
_____

Intended place of study   ☐ university   ☐ other

Level

Academic environments you expect to be in

- ☐ classroom
- ☐ laboratory
- ☐ workshop
- ☐ lecture room
- ☐ seminar/tutorial
- ☐ private study/library
- ☐ other _____

Examples of courses required for your post-graduate program

1._____ 4._____

2._____ 5._____

3._____ 6._____

Do you expect to study in any other country besides Canada?

   ☐ Yes   ☐ No

If yes, please specify _____

D. FUTURE CAREER

Where do you expect to work?

- ☐ business   ☐ academic environment
- ☐ government   ☐ other
- ☐ industry

What do you expect your duties to be (brief description)

_____

_____

Do you expect to use English in your career? ☐ Yes ☐ No

If 'Yes', will English be required   ☐ regularly
                                                ☐ often?
                                                ☐ occasionally?
                                                  ☐ seldom?

How many hours per day/week do you expect to use English?

_____ hours per _____

In what ways do you expect to use English in your career?

- ☐ speaking   ☐ face-to-face
-                              ☐ telephone/radio/television
- ☐ listening   ☐ face-to-face

☐ reading

☐ telephone/radio/television
☐ magazines
☐ professional journals
☐ reports
☐ newspapers
☐ textbooks
☐ letters

☐ writing

☐ magazine articles
☐ professional journal papers
☐ reports
☐ textbooks
☐ letters

With whom do you expect to be using English in your career?

☐ colleagues
☐ students
☐ members of the community at large

E. GENERAL INTERESTS AND ACTIVITIES where you would use English (details welcomed)

☐ entertainment at home (radio, T.V. etc.)
☐ friends, social gatherings (parties, etc.)
☐ films
☐ theatre
☐ music
☐ cultural interests
☐ travel
☐ sports
☐ community activities
☐ transportation
☐ shopping
☐ reading newspapers
☐ other needs_____

F. MISCELLANEOUS

Do you want your spouse to learn
English?   ☐ Yes ☐ No ☐ N/A
Do you want your children to learn
English?   ☐ Yes ☐ No ☐ N/A

Are there any English-speaking
people in your family?   ☐ Yes ☐ No
How many English-speaking people do you know? _____
Do they use English   ☐   regularly?
                       ☐   often
                       ☐   occasionally?
                       ☐   seldom?

Appendix IV:

Report on a Needs Survey and a Description of Purpose for an EAP Course

Adult ESL Learners. Three Pre-university Intensive Courses, Given in a University Setting

English Language Program, Carleton University, Ottawa.
Academic Year 1979–80

(Based on an adaptation of Munby, 1978)

THE SERIES of courses consists of three 12-week courses, each of which meets for 3 hours of formal instruction Monday to Friday. In addition practice in the language laboratory (on an individual, unmonitored basis) is provided. Some tutoring (individual or in small groups) is generally available. There are limited extra-curricular activities. The language of the community is of course English; there are, therefore, numerous extra-curricular opportunities for exposure to the language, both on the university campus and off it.

The courses run from mid-September to early December; from early January to the end of March or early April; and from mid-May to mid-August.

1. Purposive domain and setting
    1.1 *Participants*
        1.1.1 Identity: Age range: 17–30
                            Sex: Male and female
                            Nationality: (an analysis was given separately)
                            Place of residence: Ottawa

1.1.2 Language:

    1.1.2.1   L1: Native Languages January–April 1979
                 Arabic 18 students; Chinese 3; French 2;
                 Italian 1; Japanese 2; Ouslof (Senegal) 1;
                 Persian 5; Russian 2; Spanish 18; Thai 2;
                 Turkish 1; Vietnamese 2

    1.1.2.2   Command of English at entry:
                 In 21.115: false beginners, elementary
                 In 21.155: lower and upper intermediate
                 In 21.195: advanced

    1.1.2.3   Entry and Exit Criteria
                 Criteria for entry and exit levels to be worked
                 out in terms of linguistic forms and communi-
                 cative functions, as well as expected scores on
                 TOEFL and other tests

1.2 *Purpose domain*

    1.2.1 Course no. 27.115 'Survival' English

    1.2.2 Course 27.155 and 27.195—English for Specific
    Purposes
                 Educational, discipline-based

    1.2.2.1   Educational purpose: academic discipline
                 classification as follows (disciplines ranked in
                 most likely order of frequency of demand;
                 course design may be altered to emphasize
                 any one of these):
                 —physical science
                 —mathematics
                 —biological science
                 —engineering
                 —social science
                 —education
                 —humanities

1.3 *Setting*

    1.3.1 *Physical setting—spatial*
           Location: Ottawa
           Place: Places of general activity, daily life:
                                 city

> shops
> services
> social intercourse
> campus
> shops
> services
> social intercourse
> country/outdoors
> > limited concentration
> travel
> > limited concentration

Places of study:

> university
> lecture room/theater
> classroom
> lab
> seminar/tutorial
> private/study/library

English acquired will be for international, national or local use, depending on nationality of student.

1.3.2 *Physical setting: temporal*

Frequency and duration: Receptive use almost constant while in Canada, diminishing when participants return home. Productive use might be limited to in-class participation and production of written assignments, with limited use in daily life. If use extends beyond these parameters, it is primarily the responsibility of the student to develop the necessary skills. This syllabus will emphasize the most immediate needs in 1.3.1 above.

1.3.3 *Psychosocial setting*

—Culturally different from their own environment
—Intellectual, educationally developed, para-
    professional
—Technically sophisticated and urban
—Public uses (occasional private use)
—Unfamiliar physical settings to some extent

—Unfamiliar human settings also to some extent
—Quiet atmosphere; demanding, yet unhurried
(library research, etc.)
—Semi-formal (informal outside class) style,
both authoritarian and unauthoritarian roles,
serious and reserved behavior expected

2. *Communication needs: interaction and instrumentality.*

Interaction

2.1 Position: university student
2.2 Role set: other students, individual/in groups
professors, individual
all adult, mixed sexes, many nationalities
2.3 Social relationships: generally speaking,
subordinate–superior and equal–equal

Instrumentality

2.4 Medium: spoken: receptive
spoken: productive
written: receptive
written: productive

2.5 Mode: Close specification not necessary. Note that in this syllabus a good deal of emphasis placed on the *mono-logue* (both 'spoken to be heard', i.e. the lecture, and 'written to be read' i.e. the textbook and journal) as well as on the *dialogue* ('spoken to be heard, i.e. as in conversation and discussion)

Other possible categories are of considerably less importance

2.6 Channel: face-to-face (unilateral)
face-to-face (bilateral)
print (unilateral)
telephone (limited use)

2.7 Non-verbal medium. Some inclusion of work in the categories below:

2.7.1   Unlabelled illustrations, charts, signs
2.7.2   Mathematical and scientific symbols

2.7.3   Personal (dress, interactional proximity)
2.7.4   Kinesic
2.7.5   Paralinguistic

3. *Communication Needs: Dialect and Target Level.*

   3.1 Dialect
   Input: Standard English, General American, some RP
   Output: Standard English, General American

   3.2 *Target Level.* (See Entry and Exit criteria in 1.1.2 also)
   These are specified for each course on the attached sheets
   labelled 3.2 Target Level.

4. *Communicative events and communicative key.*

   4.1 At the basic level, the events are those of daily life: shopping,
   renting a room, ordering food, etc. These remain to be more
   closely specified.

   At the mid-point of the basic level, events common in academic
   life are to be included: discussion with other students in a
   seminar, participation in meetings, etc. These too remain to be
   specified.

   4.2 Referential vocabulary will also be filled out, especially for the
   science students, in cooperation with colleagues in the Faculty
   of Science.

   4.3 Communicative key. While this is important in that choice of
   key affects the selection of exponents for the expression of
   micro-functions, it need not be specified too closely at the
   present stage of syllabus development. It will be coordinated
   with Activities (4.1) in the production of teaching materials.

5. *Language skills selection.*

   (A list of micro-functions and of language skills was appended. The
   selection was specified for each level.)

Appendix V:

Tracking Grids

THREE examples only are provided. Any two components of a given syllabus can be mapped or tracked with simple grids of the kind shown below; use of a computer would of course permit much faster work.

TRACKING GRID I: *Rolesets and Topics*

Interlocutors§ \ Topic*	Personal Identification	House and home	Trade, profession, Occupation	Free time Entertainment	Travel	Relations with other people	Health and welfare	Education	Shopping	Food and drink	Services	Places	Languages	Weather
Stranger														
Policeman														
Teacher														
Doctor														
Employer														
Neighbour														
Friend														
Etc.														

Place a checkmark in the ☐ to indicate what topics might be talked about with which interlocutors.
Similar grids may be used for the written mode.

* This is the range of topics given in Threshold Level. Each is broken down quite finely; for each topic, a separate grid can be made.

§ Interlocutors can be specified for a group of students, or a grid may be filled out for each learner individually.

TRACKING GRID 2: *Combining Exercises (or exercise types) and Rhetorical, Discourse and Study Skills (this example provides a mixed selection)*

Exercises (or Types)*	Unit 1: Skimming & scanning	Unit 2: Recording information	Unit 3: Organizing information	Unit 4: Extracting salient points to summarize	Unit 5: Expanding relevant points into a summary
E_1					
E_2					
E_3					
E_4					
E_5 etc.					

Place a checkmark in the appropriate cells and/or use the squares to record relevant classroom materials.

* Exercise types could be listed for oral and/or written discourse (e.g. role-play, simulation, games, problem solving etc.)

TRACKING GRID 3: *Language Program Modification (Mapping a current syllabus (Compare Checklists BI, BII, Appendix II))*

	Now included		Level or	Materials
	Yes	No	Course	used
Language Functions				
A. *Expressing truth values*				
1. Factual information				
2. Argument				
3. Likelihood				
4. Attitude to truth				
5. Seeking information				
B. *Discourse skills*				
1. Cohesion of text				
2. Rhetorical cohesion				
3. Operations on a text				
4. Rhetorical organization of discourse				
5. Overt transactional skills in spoken discourse				

On this Grid, only a few functions and discourse skills are shown. The syllabus designer would need to decide how extensive a mapping would be required, and prepare his own grids accordingly.

References

Abbreviations

AVLJ: Audio Visual Language Journal
CMLR: Canadian Modern Language Review
FLA: Foreign Language Annals
IRAL: International Review of Applied Linguistics
MLJ: Modern Language Journal

Alexander, L. G. (1975) "Some Methodological Implications of *Waystage* and *Threshold Level.*" Appendix to both *Threshold Level* and *Waystage* (van Ek, 1975 and 1977).

Alexander, L. G. (1979) "A functional–notional approach to course design. *AVLJ,* **17,** pp.109–113.

Alexander, L. G., Allen, W. S., Close, R. A. and O'Neill, R. J. (1975) *English Grammatical Structure: A General Syllabus for Teachers.* London: Longman.

Allen, J. P. B. (1977) "Structural and functional models in language teaching." *TESL Talk,* **8/**1, pp.5–15.

Allen, J. P. B. (1979) "Professional development and materials models for ESL." Paper presented at the 1979 TESL Ontario Conference, November, 1979. Mimeo.

Allen, J. P. B. (1980) "A three-level curriculum model for second-language education." Mimeo. Modern Language Centre, Ontario Institute for Studies in Education.

Allen, J. P. B. and Howard, J. (1981) "Subject-related ESL: an experiment in communicative language teaching." *CMLR,* **37,** pp.535–550.

Allen, J. P. B. and Widdowson, H. G. (1974a) "Teaching the communicative use of English." *IRAL,* **12,** pp.1–21.

Allen, J. P. B. and Widdowson, H. G. (1974b) *English in Focus Series.* London: Oxford University Press.

Allwright, R. (1978) "Abdication and responsibility in language teaching." Paper prepared for the 1978 Berne Colloquium on Applied Linguistics. Mimeo.

Allwright, R. (1979) "Language learning through communication practice." In Brumfit and Johnson (1979), pp.167–182.

Anthony, E. M. (1972) "Approach, method and technique." In Allen and Campbell (eds) (1972) *Teaching English as a Second language.* New York: McGraw-Hill, (2nd edn), pp.4–8.

Asher, J. J. (1977) *Learning Another Language Through Actions: The Complete Teacher's Guidebook.* Los Gatos, California: Sky Oaks Productions.

Austin, J. L. (1961) *Philosophical Papers.* London: Oxford University Press.

Austin, J. L. (1962) *How to Do Things With Words.* London: Oxford University Press.

Bachman, L. F. and Strick, G. J. (1981) "An analytical approach to language program design." In Mackay and Palmer (1981), pp.45–63.

Belanger, B. (1978) *La Suggestologie: Les théories revolutionnaires du Dr. Lozanov et leurs applications.* Paris: Retz.

Bibeau, G. (1976) *Report of the Independent Study on the Language Training Programmes of the Public Service of Canada.* Ottawa: Language Training Programmes of the Public Service of Canada.

Bibeau, G. (1979) "Nouveaux besoins en formation des professeurs de langue seconde." *Actes du Colloque la Formation des Maîtres.* In Numéro spécial, *Journal de l'Institut de langues vivantes,* Université d'Ottawa (1979), pp.11–21.

Bloom, B. S. *et al.* (1975) *Taxonomy of Educational Objectives: The Classification of Educational Goals, Handbook 1: Cognitive Domain.* New York: David McKay.

Born, W. (ed.) (1975) *Goals Clarification: Curriculum Teaching Evaluation.* Report of the Working Committees. Northeast Conference on the Teaching of Foreign Languages.

Bott, D. E. (1981) "Notions and functions across cultures." *English Teaching Forum,* **19**, pp.28–32.

British Council (1970) *ELT Guide No. 1—Communication Games.* Windsor, England: NFER Publishing Company.

Britton, J. (1970) *Language and Learning.* Harmondsworth: Penguin.

Brumfit, C. (1980a) *Problems and Principles in English Teaching.* Oxford: Pergamon Press.

Brumfit, C. (1980b) "From defining to designing: communicative specifications versus communicative methodology in foreign-language teaching." In Müller (ed.), *The Foreign Language Syllabus and Communicative Approaches to Teaching: Proceedings of a European-American Seminar.* Special issue of *Studies in Second-Language Acquisition,* pp.1–9.

Brumfit, C. (1981) "Notional syllabuses revisited: a response." *Applied Linguistics,* **2**, pp.90–92.

Brumfit, C. J. and Johnson, K. (1979) *The Communicative Approach to Language Teaching.* London: Oxford University Press.

Bruton, C. J., Candlin, C. N. and Leather, J. H. (1976) "Doctor speech functions in casualty consultations: predictable structures of discourse in a regulated setting." In Nikel (ed.), *Proceedings of the Fourth International Congress of Applied Linguistics,* Stuttgart, Hochshul Verlag, *Vol. 1,* pp.297–312.

Canale, M. and Swain, M. (1980) "Theoretical bases of communicative approaches to second-language teaching and testing." *Applied Linguistics,* **1**, pp.1–47.

Candlin, C. N. (1973) "The status of pedagogical grammars." In Corder and Roulet (eds), *Theoretical Linguistic Models in Applied Linguistics.* Paris: Didier, pp.55–64.

Candlin, C. N. (1974) "An approach to treating extratextual function in a language teaching syllabus." In Corder and Roulet (eds), *Linguistic Insights in Applied Linguistics.* Paris: Didier, pp.107–117.

Candlin, C. N. (1976) "Communicative language teaching and the debt to pragmatics." In Rameh (ed.) *Georgetown University Round Table on Languages and Linguistics.* Washington, D. C.: Georgetown University Press, pp.237–256. Georgetown University Monograph Series in Language Learning.

Candlin, C. N. (ed.) (1981) *The Communicative Teaching of English: Principles and an Exercise Typology.* Harlow, Essex: Longman.

Candlin, C. N. and Breen, M. P. (1979) "Evaluating and designing language-teaching materials." *Practical Papers in English Language Education,* **2**, pp.172–216. University of Lancaster.

Candlin, C. N., Bruton, C. J. and Leather, J. H. (1976) "Doctors in casualty: specialist-course design from a data base." *IRAL,* **14**, pp.245–272.

Carroll, B. J. (1980) *Testing Communicative Performance: An Interim Study.* Oxford: Pergamon Press.

Carroll, J. B. (1965) "The contributions of psychological theory and educational research to the teaching of foreign languages." *Modern Language Journal,* **49**, pp.273–281.

Carroll, J. B. (1966) "Research in foreign language teaching: the last five years." *Language Teaching: Broader Contexts.* Report of the Working Committees, Northeast Conference on the Teaching of Foreign Languages. New York: pp.12–42.

Chastain, K. D. (1970) "A methodological study comparing the audio-lingual habit theory and the cognitive code-learning theory—a continuation. *MLJ*, **54**, pp.257-265.

Chastain, K. D. (1976) *Developing Second-language Skills* (2nd edn), Chicago: Rand-McNally College Publishing Co.

Chastain, K. D. and Woerdehoff, F. J. (1968) "A methodological study comparing the audio-lingual habit theory and the cognitive code-learning theory." *MLJ*, **52**, pp.268-279.

Chomsky, N. (1965) *Aspects of the Theory of Syntax*. Cambridge, MA: The MIT Press.

Clark, J. L. (1979) "The syllabus. What should the learner learn?" *AVLJ*, **17**, pp.99-108.

Corder, S. Pit (1967) "The significance of learners' errors." *IRAL*, **5**, pp.161-169.

Corder, S. Pit (1972) "Problems and solutions in applied linguistics." In Qvistgaard, Schwarz and Spang-Hanssen (eds), *Proceedings of the Third International Congress of Applied Linguistics*. Copenhagen, **Vol. III**. Heidelberg: Julius Groos Verlag, pp.3-23.

Corder, S. Pit (1973) *Introducing Applied Linguistics*. Harmondsworth: Penguin.

Corder, S. Pit (1978a) "Language-learner language." In Richards (ed.), *Understanding Second and Foreign Language Learning*. Rowley, MA: Newbury House, Inc., pp.71-93.

Corder, S. Pit (1978b) "Trends in EFL." *SPEAQ Journal*, **2**/4, pp.11-23.

Coste, D. *et al.* (1976) *Un niveau-seuil*. Strasbourg: Council of Europe.

Coulthard, M. (1977) *An Introduction to Discourse Analysis*. London: Longman.

Courchêne, R. (1981) "The history of the term 'applied' in applied linguistics." In Savard, and Laforge (eds), *Proceedings of the 5th Congress of L'Association internationale de linguistique appliqué*. Québec: Presses de l'Université Laval, pp.66-88.

Cummins, J. (1976) "The influence of bilingualism on cognitive growth." *Working Papers on Bilingualism*, No. 9: pp.1-43.

Cummins, J. (1978) "The cognitive development of children in immersion programs." *CMLR*, **34**, pp.855-883.

Cummins, J. (1979) "Linguistic interdependence and the educational development of bilingual children." *Review of Educational Research*, **49**, pp.222-251.

Curran, C. A. (1976) *Counseling-Learning in Second-Languages*. Apple River, IL: Apple River Press.

Currie, W. B. (1975) "European syllabuses in English as a foreign language." *Language Learning*, **25**, pp.339-354.

DeByser, F. (1980) "Expressing Disagreement." In Müller (ed.), *The Foreign Language Syllabus and Communicative Approaches to Teaching*. Special issue of *Studies in Second-Language Acquisition*, **3**, pp.42-56.

Dik, S. C. (1978) *Functional Grammar*. Amsterdam: North Holland Publishing Co.

Diller, K. (1978) *The Language Teaching Controversy*. Rowley, MA: Newbury House.

Dixson, R. J. (1973) *Modern American English. Book I*. Revised edn, Montreal: Centre Educatif et Culturel, Inc.

Dobson, J. M. (1979) "The notional syllabus: theory and practice." *English Teaching Forum*, **17**/2, pp.2-10.

Dos Gahli, D. and Tremblay, D. (1980) "Projet d'elaboration d'un cours de français au niveau avancé, destiné aux diplomates canadiens." *CMLR*, **36**, pp.434-443.

English Language Teaching Development Unit (ELTDU) of Oxford University Press (1976) *Stages of Attainment Scale and Test Battery: General Information*. London: Oxford University Press.

Finnochiaro, M. (1978) "Notional–functional syllabuses: 1978 part III." In Blatchford and Schacter (eds) *On TESOL '78: Policies, Programs, Practices.* Washington, DC: TESOL, pp.24–32.

Finocchiaro, M. (1979) "The functional–notional syllabus: promise, problems, practices." *English Teaching Forum,* 17/2, pp.11–20.

Firth, J. R. (1968) *Selected Papers: 1952-59.* Edited by Palmer, F. R., London: Longmans, Green & Co.

Fraser, B. (1978) "Acquiring social competence in a second language." *RELC Journal,* 9, pp.1–21.

Freedman, A., Pringle, I. and Yalden, J. (forthcoming) *Learning to Write: First Language, Second language.* London: Longman.

Gattegno, C. (1972) *Teaching Foreign Languages in School the Silent Way* (2nd edn), New York: Educational Editions.

Gattegno, C. (1976) *The Common Sense of Teaching Foreign Languages.* New York: Educational Solutions.

Germain, C. (1979) "La contextualisation dans l'enseignement des langues secondaires et de la langue maternelle." *Actes, 10e Colloque,* Association canadienne de linguistique appliquée. Montréal: ACLA, pp.7–30.

Germain, C. (1980) "L'approche fonctionnelle en didactique des langues." *CMLR,* 37, pp.10–24.

Gouvernement du Québec (1980) "Programmes d'études. Anglais et français langues secondes." Québec: Ministère de l'éducation. Direction générale du développement pédagogique.

Grellet, F. (1981) *Developing Reading Skills: A Practical Guide to Reading Comprehension Exercises.* New York: Cambridge University Press.

Guillo, P. and Creus, L. (1977) "Nouvelles orientations en didactique des langues." *Echanges* 9, August.

Guntermann, G. (1980) "Factors in targeting proficiency levels and an approach to 'real' and 'realistic' practice." In Müller, *The Foreign Language Syllabus and Communicative Approaches to Teaching: Proceedings of a European–American Seminar.* Special issue of *Studies in Second-Language Acquisition,* pp.34–41.

Guntermann, G. and Phillips, J. K. (1981) "Communicative course design: developing functional ability in all four skills." *CMLR,* 37, pp.329–343.

Halliday, M. A. K. (1973) *Explorations in the Functions of Language.* London: Edward Arnold.

Halliday, M. A. K. (1975) *Learning How to Mean: Explorations in the Development of Language.* London: Edward Arnold.

Halliday, M. A. K. (1976) *System and Function in Language.* London: Oxford University Press.

Halliday, M. A. K. (1978) *Language as Social Semiotic.* London: Edward Arnold.

Halliday, M. A. K. and Hasan, R. (1976) *Cohesion in English.* London: Longman.

Harlow, L. L., Flint-Smith, W. and Garfinkel, A. (1980) "Student-perceived communication needs: infrastructure of the functional–notional syllabus." *FLA,* 13, pp.11–22.

Hill, C. P. (1975) "Review of van Ek, *Threshold Level.*" *ELT Journal,* 31/4, pp.334–335.

Hill, L. A. (1967) *Selected Articles on the Teaching of English as a Foreign Language.* London: Oxford University Press.

Holden, S. (ed.) (1978) *Visual Aids for Classroom Interaction.* London: Modern English Publications.

Holec, H. (1980a) "Learner-centered communicative language teaching: needs analysis revisited." In Müller, *The Foreign Language Syllabus and Communicative Approaches to Teaching: Proceedings of a European–American Seminar.* Special issue of *Studies in Second-Language Acquisition,* pp.26–33.

Holec, H. (1980b) *Autonomy and Foreign Language Learning.* Strasbourg: Council of Europe.

Holenstein, E. (1976) *Roman Jakobson's Approach to Language: Phenomenological Structuralism.* Translated by C. Schelbert and T. Schelbert. Bloomington, IN: Indiana University Press.

Hymes, D. (1970) "The ethnography of speaking." In Fishman (ed.) *Readings in the Sociology of Language.* The Hague: Mouton.

Hymes, D. (1972) "On communicative competence." In Pride and Holmes (eds.) *Sociolinguistics,* pp.269–293.

Jakobson, R. (1960) "Closing statement: linguistics and poetics." In Seboek (ed.), *Style in Language.* Cambridge, MA: MIT Press, pp.350–377.

Johnson, K. (1977a) "The adoption of functional syllabuses for general courses. *CMLR,* **33,** pp.667–680.

Johnson, K. (1977b) "Adult beginners: a functional or just a communicative approach?" Paper delivered at the B.A.A.L. Annual General Meeting, Colchester, September 1977. Reprinted in Johnson, 1982, *Communicative Syllabus Design and Methodology.* Oxford: Pergamon Press.

Johnson, K. (1980) " 'Systematic' and 'non-systematic' components in a communicative approach to language teaching." Paper delivered at the Berne Colloquium, June 1980. Mimeographed.

Johnson, K. (1982) *Communicative Syllabus Design and Methodology.* Oxford: Pergamon Press.

Jupp, T. C. and Hodlin, S. (1975) *Industrial English: An Example of Theory and Practice in Functional Language Teaching.* London: Heinemann Educational.

Kaplan, R. (ed.) (1980) *On the Scope of Applied Linguistics.* Rowley, MA: Newbury House.

Krashen, S. D. (1978) "Adult second-language acquisition and learning: a review of theory and applications." Mimeographed.

Krashen, S. D. (1981) *Second-Language Acquisition and Second-Language Learning.* Oxford: Pergamon Press.

Krashen, S. D. (in press) *Principles and Practice in Second-language Acquisition.*

Kress, G. (ed.) (1976) *Halliday: System and Function in Language.* London: Oxford University Press.

Lackstrom, J., Selinker, L. and Trimble, L. P., (1970) "Grammar and technical English." in Lugton (ed.), *English as a Second-Language: Current Issues.* Philadelphia: The Center for Curriculum Development, pp.101–134.

Lado, R. (1964) *Language Teaching: A Scientific Approach.* New York: McGraw-Hill, Inc.

Lado, R. (1970) *Lado English Series. Book I.* Montréal: Centre Educatif et Cultural Inc.

Larsen-Freeman, D. (1980) *Discourse Analysis in Second-language Research.* Rowley, MA: Newbury House.

Leech, G. and Svartvik, J. (1975) *A Communicative Grammar of English.* London: Longman.

Lenneberg, E. (1967) *Biological Foundations of Language.* New York: Wiley.

Lewis, E. G. (1974) *Linguistics and Second-Language Pedagogy: A Theoretical Study.* The Hague: Mouton.

Littlewood, W. T. (1978) "Communicative language teaching." *AVLJ,* 16: 131–136.

194   References

Mackay, R. (1978) "Practical curriculum development and evalution in ESP/EST." *EST Newsletter*, No. 20 (November, 1978), pp.2–5.
Mackay, R. (1979) "Teaching the information-gathering skills." In Mackay, Barkman and Jordan, *Reading in a Second-Language*. Rowley, MA: Newbury House, pp.79–90.
Mackay, R., Barkman, B. and Jordan, R. R. (eds) (1979) *Reading in a Second-Language*. Rowley, MA: Newbury House.
Mackay, R. and Mountford, A. (1976) "Pedagogic alternatives to 'Explication de texte' as a procedure for teaching reading comprehension with special reference to English for science and technology." Bulletin Pedagogique of the Institut Universitaires de Technologie (October 1976), p.44.
Mackay, R. and Mountford, A. (eds) (1978) *English for Specific Purposes*. London: Longman.
Mackay, R. and Palmer, J. D. (eds) (1981) *Languages for Specific Purposes: Program Design and Evaluation*. Rowley, MA: Newbury House.
Mackey, W. F. (1965) *Language Teaching Analysis*. London: Longmans, Green & Co.
Mackey, W. F. (1977) *The Contextual Revolt in Language Training: Its Theoretical Foundations*. Québec: International Centre for Research in Bilingualism.
Maley, A. (1980) "Teaching for communicative competence: illusion and reality." In Müller, *The Foreign Language Syllabus and Communicative Approaches to Teaching: Proceedings of a European–American Seminar*. Special issue of *Studies in Second-Language Acquisition*, pp.11–16.
Malinowski, B. (1923) "The problem of meaning in primitive languages." In Ogden and Richards, *The Meaning of Meaning*. London: Routledge and Kegan Paul. (8th edn. 1946), pp.296–336.
Mareschal, R. (ed.) (1977) *Needs Oriented Language Teaching. CMLR,* **5,** Special Issue.
Martin, M. A. (1978) "The application of spiralling to the teaching of grammar." *TESOL Quarterly*, **12**/2.
McDonough, J. (undated) "Report on a syllabus in EAP for the Ayacucho program." Mimeographed.
Mills, G. (1978) "The integration of grammar-teaching into the communicative curriculum: problems and issues." *Bulletin de l'Acla*, **2**/3, pp.21–26.
Mohan, B. (1977) "Toward a situational curriculum." In Brown, Yorio and Crymes (eds), *Teaching and Learning English as a Second-Language: Trends in Research and Practice. On TESL '77*.
Moirand, S. (1981) L'enseignement de la langue comme instrument de communication: état de la question." In *Bulletin de l'Acla*, Automne, 1981. Actes du 12e Colloque Annuel, pp.11–34.
Morrow, K. E. (1977a) "Teaching the functions of language." *English Language Teaching Journal*, **32**/1, pp.9–14.
Morrow, K. E. (1977b) *Techniques of Evaluation for a Notional Syllabus*. Royal Society of Arts.
Moskowitz, G. (1978) "Dare to share: humanistic techniques in the second-language class." *SPEAQ Journal*, **4,** pp.25–33.
Munby, J. (1978) *Communicative Syllabus Design*. London: Cambridge University Press.
Newmark, L. (1966) "How not to interfere with language learning." In Brumfit and Johnson (1979), *The Communicative Approach to Language Teaching*. London: Oxford University Press, pp.160–166.
Norris, W. E. (1971) *TESOL at the Beginning of the '70s: Trends, Topics and Research*

Needs. Pittsburgh: Department of Linguistics and University Centre for International Studies, University of Pittsburgh.

Ogden, C. K. and Richards, I. A. (1946) *The Meaning of Meaning.* London: Routledge and Kegan Paul. (8th edn).

Oller, J. W. Jr. (1973) "Some psycholinguistic controversies." In Oller, Jr. and Richards (eds), *Focus on the learner,* pp.36–52. Rowley, MA: Newbury House.

Oller, J. W. Jr. and Richards J. C. (eds) (1973) *Focus on the Learner* Rowley, MA: Newbury House.

O'Neill, R. (1970) *English in Situations.* London: Oxford University Press.

Orem, R. (1981) "Entering the '80s—some professional perspectives." *TESOL Newsletter,* **15**/2: p.1–3.

Paulston, C. B. (1981) "Notional syllabuses revisited: some comments." *Applied Linguistics,* **2**, pp.93–95.

Paulston, C. B. and Bruder, M. (1976) *Teaching English as a Second Language: Techniques and Procedures.* Cambridge, MA: Winthrop Publishers, Inc.

Penfield, W. C. and Roberts, L. (1959) *Speech and Brain Mechanisms.* New Jersey: Princeton University Press.

Pierson, H. D. and Friederichs, J. (1981) "Curriculum planning for ESL students at the university." *English Teaching Forum,* **19**/3, pp.30–35.

Politzer, R. (1965) *Teaching French: An Introduction to Applied Linguistics.* New York: Blaisdell Publishing Co.

Praninskas, J. (1975) *A Rapid Review of English Grammar.* (2nd edn). Englewood Cliffs, NJ: Prentice-Hall, Inc.

Quirk, R. and Greenbaum, S. (1973) *A University Grammar of English.* London: Longman.

RELC (1979) "Guidelines for communication activities." *RELC Journal.* Supplement No. 1.

Richards, J. C. (1973) "Error analysis and second-language strategies." In Richards, (ed.), *Focus on the learner: Pragmatic Perspectives for the Language Teacher.* Rowley, MA: Newbury House Inc., pp.114–135.

Richterich, R. (1979) "L'antidéfinition des besoins langagiers comme pratique pédagogique." *Les Français dans le monde* **149**, pp.54–58.

Richterich, R. *et al.* (1981) "Préoccupations actuelles des chercheurs européens en didactique des langues." In *Bulletin de l'Acla,* Automne, 1981. Actes du 12e colloque annuel, pp.195–207.

Richterich, R. and Chancerel, J.-L. (1980) *Identifying the Needs of Adults Learning a Foreign Language.* Oxford: Pergamon Press.

Rivers, W. (1964) *The Psychologist and the Foreign Language Teacher.* Chicago: University of Chicago Press.

Rivers, W. (1980) "Foreign language acquisition: where the real problems lie." *Applied Linguistics,* **1**, pp.48–59.

Robertson, A. S. (1971) "Curriculum building." In Deighton (ed.), *International Encyclopedia of Education.* New York: MacMillan.

Robins, R. H. (1967) *A Short History of Linguistics.* London: Longman.

Robinson, P. (1980) *ESP (English for Specific Purposes).* Oxford: Pergamon Press.

Roulet, E. (1975) *Linguistic Theory, Linguistic Description and Language Teaching.* Translated by C. N. Candlin. London: Longman.

Schlesinger, I. M. (1977) *Production and Comprehension of Utterances.* Hillsdale, NJ: Lawrence Erlbaum Associates.

Schutz, N. W. and Derwing, B. L. (1981) "The problem of needs assessment in English for specific purposes: some theoretical and practical considerations." In Mackay and Darwin Palmer (eds), *Languages for Specific Purposes: Program Design and Evaluation.* Rowley, MA: Newbury House, pp.29–44.

Searle, J. (1969) *Speech Acts.* London: Cambridge University Press.

Searle, J. (1971) *The Philosophy of Language.* London: Oxford University Press.

Searle, J. (1975) "Indirect speech acts." In Cole and Morgan (eds), *Syntax and Semantics,* Vol. **3,** *Speech Acts.* New York: Academic Press.

Selinker, L. (1972) "Interlanguage." *IRAL,* **10,** pp.219–231.

Selinker, L., Todd-Trimble, R. M., and Trimble, L. (1976) "Presuppositional rhetorical information in EST discourse." *TESOL Quarterly,* **10,** pp.281–290.

Selinker, L., Todd-Trimble, M. and Trimble, L. (1978) "Rhetorical function shifts in EST discourse." *TESOL Quarterly,* **12,** pp.311–320.

Shaw, A. M. (1975) "Approaches to a communicative syllabus in foreign language curriculum development." Ph. D. Dissertation: University of Essex.

Shaw, A. M. (1977) "Foreign-language syllabus development: some recent approaches." *Language Teaching and Linguistics: Abstracts,* **10**/4, pp.217–233.

Shaw, P. (1979) "Classroom materials and techniques in the notional–functional approach." Paper presented at the 13th Annual TESOL Conference, San Francisco, March 1979.

Sinclair, J. M. and Coulthard, M. (1975) *Towards an Analysis of Discourse: the English Used by Teachers and Pupils.* London: Oxford University Press.

Spolsky, B. (1978) *Educational Linguistics: an Introduction.* Rowley, MA: Newbury House.

Steiner, F. (1970) "Performance objectives in the teaching of foreign languages." *Foreign Language Annals,* **3**/4, pp.579–591.

Stern, H. H. (1972) "Directions in language teaching theory and research." In Qvistgaard, Schwarz and Sprang-Hanssen (eds), *Proceedings of the Third International Congress of Applied Linguistics, Copenhagen, 1972.* Heidelberg: Julius Groos Verlag, Vol. **III,** pp.61–108.

Stern, H. H. (1978) "The formal–functional distinction in language pedagogy: A conceptual clarification." In Savard and Laforge (eds), *Proceedings of the 5th International Congress of Applied Linguistics.* Québec: Les Presses de l'Université Laval, pp.425–455.

Stevick, E. (1971) *Memory, Meaning and Method.* Rowley, MA: Newbury House. Publishers.

Stratton, F. (1977) "Putting the communicative syllabus in its place." *TESOL Quarterly,* **11**/2, pp.131–141.

Strevens, P. (1977) *New Orientations in the Teaching of English.* London: Oxford University Press.

Strevens, P. (1978) "Special Purpose Language Teaching: A Perspective," *Language Teaching and Linguistics: Abstracts* II: p.156.

Strevens, P. (1980) "English for special purposes: an analysis and survey." In Croft, *Readings in English as a Second Language,* pp.458–472. (2nd edn). Cambridge, MA: Winthrop Inc.

Terrell, T. D. (1977) "A natural approach to second-language acquisition and learning." *MLJ;* **61,** pp.325–337.

Trim, J. L. M. (1973) "Draft outline of a European unit/credit system for modern language learning by adults." In *Systems Development in Adult Language Learning,* pp.15–28. Strasbourg: Council of Europe.

Trim, J. L. M. (1978a) "A European unit/credit system." In *A European Unit/Credit System for Modern Language Learning by Adults,* pp.2–4. Strasbourg: Council of Europe.

Trim, J. L. M. (1978b) "Some possible lines of development of an overall structure for a European unit/credit scheme for foreign language learning by adults." Strasbourg: Council of Europe.

Trim, J. L. M. (1980) "The Council of Europe modern language project as an example of European cooperation." In van Deth and Puyo (eds), *Langues et coopération européenne.* Actes du colloque international Strasbourg 1979). Paris: Cireel.

Trim, J. L. M. (1981) "The modern language project of the Council of Europe: findings and prospects." Mimeographed Summary. Urbino, 10 September 1981.

Trim, J. L. M., Richterich, R., van Ek, J. and Wilkins, D. (1973) *Systems Development in Adult Language Learning.* Strasbourg: Council of Europe.

United Nations Educational, Scientific and Cultural Organization (UNESCO) (1975) ED-75/CONF.606/5 Working paper: "Meeting of experts on diversification of methods and techniques for teaching a second or foreign language with reference to the aims in view, levels and age groups, social and professional background."

Urbancic, A. (1979) "The city: a new approach to conversation classes." *CMLR,* **36**/1, pp.97–104.

Vachek, J. (1972) "The linguistic theory of the Prague school." In Fried (ed.), *The Prague School of Linguistics and Language Teaching.* London: Oxford University Press, pp.11–28.

Valdman, A. (1978) "Communicative use of language and syllabus design." *FLA,* **11**, pp.567–578.

Valdman, A. (1980) "Communicative ability and syllabus design for global foreign language courses." In Müller (ed.), *The Foreign Language Syllabus and Communicative Approaches to Teaching: Proceedings of a European/American seminar.* Special issue of *Studies in Second-Language Acquisition,* pp.81–96.

Valette, R. and Disick, R. (1977) *Modern Language Performance Objectives and Individualization.* New York: Harcourt Brace and Jovanovich.

van Ek, J. A. (1973) "The threshold level in a unit/credit system." In Trim (ed.), *Systems Development in Adult Language Learning.* Strasbourg: Council of Europe, pp.89–146.

van Ek, J. A. (1975) *The Threshold Level.* Strasbourg: Council of Europe.

van Ek, J. A. (1976) *The Threshold Level for Modern Language Learning in Schools.* London: Longman.

van Ek, J. A. and Alexander, L. G. (1977) *Waystage.* Strasbourg: Council of Europe.

Widdowson, H. G. (1974) "An approach to the teaching of scientific English discourse." *RELC Journal,* **5**/1, pp.27–40.

Widdowson, H. G. (1978a) "Notional–functional syllabuses: 1978 Part IV." In Blatchford and Schacter (eds), *On TESOL '78: EFL Policies, Programs, Practices.* Washington, DC: TESOL, pp.33–35.

Widdowson, H. G. (1978b) "The acquisition and use of language system." Paper presented at the 1978 Berne Colloquium. Mimeographed.

Widdowson, H. G. (1979a) *Explorations in Applied Linguistics.* London: Oxford University Press.

Widdowson, H. G. (ed.) (1979b) *Reading and Thinking in English Series.* London: Oxford University Press.

Wilkinson, A. (1975) *Language and Education.* London: Oxford University Press.

Wilkins, D. A. (1974) "Notional syllabuses and the concept of a minimum adequate grammar." In Corder and Roulet (eds), *Linguistic Insights in Applied Linguistics*. Paris: Didier, pp.119–128.

Wilkins, D. A. (1976) *Notional Syllabuses*. London: Oxford University Press.

Wilkins, D. A. (1978) "Approaches to syllabus design: communicative, functional or notional." In Johnson and Morrow (eds), *Functional Material and the Classroom Teacher: Some Background Issues*. University of Reading: Centre for Applied Language Studies, pp.1–13.

Wilkins, D. A. (1981) "Communicative language teaching: some misconceptions and some proposals." In *Bulletin de l'Acla*, Automne 1981, pp.95–105. Actes du 12e colloque annuel.

Wilkinson, A. (1975) *Language and Education*. London: Oxford University Press.

Yalden, J. (1976) "Methods in language teaching." In Isbelle (ed.), *What's What for Children Learning French*. Ottawa: Citizens' Committee on Children, pp.5-11.

Yalden, J. (1980a) "Form and function: the design of a six-phase syllabus in English as a second language." *CMLR*, **36**, pp.452–460.

Yalden, J. (1980b) "The design of a balanced syllabus." Paper presented at the Conference on Second-Language Teaching and Learning. University of Western Ontario, April 1980. Mimeograph.

Young, L. and O'Brien, W. (1979) "English for academic purposes through Canadian literature and history. *CMLR*, **35**, pp.581–587.

Zobl, H. (1980) "Accommodating the categorial side of language learning in syllabus design." *TESL Talk*, **11**, pp.56–62.